E1

Davidson
1996

» LUDUS «

Medieval and Early Renaissance Theatre and Drama

1

Edited by

Wim Hüsken

Volume 1: English Parish Drama

Amsterdam - Atlanta, 1996

English Parish Drama

Edited by
Alexandra F. Johnston
and
Wim Hüsken

ⓧ The paper on which this book is printed meets the requirements of "ISO 9706:1994, Information and documentation - Paper for documents - Requirements for permanence".

ISBN: 90-420-0060-0
©Editions Rodopi B.V., Amsterdam - Atlanta, GA 1996
Printed in The Netherlands

Contents

Illustrations

The illustrations that accompany David Georges' article are taken from Alfred Burton's *Rush-Bearing*, Manchester, 1891, pp. 67, 26, and 58. Burton's many illustrations derive from various sources. 'A Lancashire Rush-Cart' first appeared in William Andrews' *Curiosities of the Church* (1890), but 'Rush-Bearing' and 'Failsworth Rush-Bearing' may be either the work of T. Oliver or from *Art Journal* or *The Graphic*. Burton praised Oliver for 'great assistance with his pencil' and also acknowledged a debt to the proprietors of the two journals for use of illustrations. In any case, it is a fair conclusion that all of Burton's illustrations are of nineteenth-century origin.

Introduction

Alexandra F. Johnston

It is more than twenty years since the serious reconsideration of the surviving documentary evidence for English drama began. The first publications of the Records of Early English Drama series, the two volumes of the records of York, have now been in print for over fifteen years.[1] These documents represent the richest vein of provincial record evidence that survives from a single location. No other single venue, not even Coventry with its greater wealth of guild records, gives us such a comprehensive picture of the dramatic, musical and ceremonial life of an English urban community outside London. Not only do we have the York records, we also have the text of the Corpus Christi play complete in all its literary complexity. Because the evidence is so full and the text so sophisticated, generations of scholars have made the mistake of extrapolating from the evidence at York to build a general picture of English drama in the late Middle Ages and early modern period. But the evidence from York has no validity beyond the jurisdiction of that city. What we are discovering as REED editors explore the surviving evidence especially from smaller and more southern towns is that York, its plays, its mode of production and its complex guild structure is unique. So are the events in Chester and Coventry. The phenomenon of civic sponsored, episodic, processional drama presenting salvation history from Creation to Doomsday performed in slightly different ways in those cities and perhaps in Beverley and Newcastle upon Tyne is not the English norm. The norm is to be found in much smaller events based in parishes and towns all over the kingdom. It is from the evidence of these smaller venues that any new history of English theatre must be extrapolated. Only when we have understood these smaller events can we properly understand the place in the complex pattern of the large and anomalous multiple episode plays.

This collection of essays begins to come to terms with the multiplicity of dramatic and para-dramatic activity that flourished in England at the parish level. Most of the essays began as papers delivered at the twenty-eighth Medieval Conference at Western Michigan University in May 1993. Other essays have been solicited to round out the volume with further examples of parish activities. All the contributors are editors in the Records of Early English Drama project and bring to their material the insights of scholars working with original material in what are still only partially charted waters. The evidence here adduced is largely from churchwardens' accounts and from the records of the ecclesiastical courts. Neither the hard-pressed wardens nor the busy ecclesiastical lawyers were primarily interested in drama or entertainment. For them, the activities were incidental to their major concern -- on the one hand the accounting of the church revenues and on the other the prosecution of individuals accused of breaking the regulations under the jurisdiction of the church courts. The church courts not only enforced the injunctions of the higher ecclesiastical courts, they heard cases which would normally be handled in the civil courts if they had taken place on church property. For example, there is a complex assault case in Newbury, Berkshire, for the year 1600 involving the local musician that was tried in the ecclesiastical court only because the assault took place in the Newbury church yard.[2] Other invaluable sources of information survive to supplement the wardens' accounts and the legal records. These are private account journals such as that of Prior More of Worcester that is the basis for David Klausner's essay, the monastic accounts of such houses as Bicester in Oxfordshire from which I have gleaned some interesting details and rare secular town records such as those used so effectively by James Gibson in his essay on the New Romney Passio Play. We must always bear in mind that whatever its origin, evidence from this period is fragmentary and often enigmatic. We are dependent upon what has survived and this is a fraction of what once existed. Peter Greenfield's essay is a model of sensible analysis based on very little material. My own work in the adjacent counties of Berkshire, Buckinghamshire and Oxfordshire has discovered a radical difference in the survival of the evidence. Berkshire and Oxfordshire are rich in records, whereas practically nothing survives from Buckinghamshire. Peter Greenfield has found much the same pattern in the counties to the east of Buckinghamshire. Whether, as is sometimes suggested, the records from these areas were destroyed after the Restoration because they reflected the religious and political views of the losing side, we will never know. What is certain is that the activities of some areas of England are fully documented while there is nothing but silence from others. Nevertheless, as the editors for the REED project share their material, a critical mass of information is growing from which is emerging a new understanding of the social context of early drama and entertainment.

The common thread tying these essays together is parish finances. Whether a parish was a large and wealthy one co-terminus with a prosperous town such as New Romney in Kent, or Thame in Oxfordshire or Tewkesbury in Gloucestershire, or a tiny cluster of houses huddled around the parish church and its yard in the depths of the countryside, each was driven by the necessity to generate sufficient income to maintain the fabric of the church. It was the obligation of the churchwardens to keep the building in repair from the chancel steps westward -- that is the nave, the side chapels, the tower, the churchyard, the gate and the church house, if any. The clergy had a similar obligation to maintain the chancel and the altar. By the time the mass of evidence begins to survive in the late fifteenth century, many of the churches, especially in the south, were already centuries old and demanded, as they do now, constant repair. The basic pattern that emerges from the evidence and is reflected in these essays is the universal existence of a parish fund-raising event with the generic name of "church ale" which took place between May Day and Midsummer most fre-

quently at Whitsun (the feast of Pentecost) and sometimes on
Corpus Christi Day eleven days later. At the ale, the parishioners
and their neighbours came together to drink, dance and entertain
themselves in various other ways. Sometimes, especially in the
north, as the essays of David George, Elizabeth Baldwin and
Barbara Palmer make clear, rushbearing was an integral part of the
event. Sometimes, in a pattern that is as yet not fully defined but
seems more prominent in the south, lords and ladies of the festival
were chosen to preside over the festivities that sometimes lasted as
long as a week. This phenomenon is discussed in my essay and
those of Peter Greenfield and Barbara Palmer. Other entertainments such as bear-baiting, biblical plays, folk plays and morris
dancing were attached to the essential money making event to attract the crowds. The local and regional customs reflected in these
essays are rich and various.

Towards the end of the sixteenth century, the ecclesiastical authorities sought to suppress these activities. In 1575, the churchwardens of St. Laurence, Reading, forced to find an alternate
source of income, decreed that

> In Consideracion That the Colleccions or gatheringes heretofore Ac-
> costomably vsed for and towardes the mayntenaunce of the Church
> As well on the feast of All saintes, The feast of the Byrthe of our
> Lord god As on Hocke Monday & Hocke Tewesdaye; Maye Daye
> And at the feast of Penticost commonly called Whytsontyde togyther
> With the Chauntery Landes ar lefte of and cleane taken from the
> Churche to the great Impoverishement therof, the which heretofore
> Dyd muche healpe the same, It is therefore of Necessytye By and
> with the Assent Concent and aggreament of the parisheners then
> And there beinge presente, for and towardes the mayntenaunce of the
> Contynuall chardges of the Churche by these presentes forener mai<.>
> Ordayned concluded vpon and fully Aggreed as hereafter followith
> That is that every Woman, that heretofore hathe byn sett by any of
> the Churchwardins, or that of them selves do or have vsed to sytt on
> the Sondayes or holydayes in any of the seates beneathe the pulpett,
> and above the southe syde, Churche doore, or in any of the Seates in
> the Mydle Raynge of seates above the saide Churche doore Shall
> yerely paye iiij d A pece for the Churche profytt & towardes the

contynuall chardges therof. At two feastes in the yere That is to say
At the feast of the Byrthe of our Lord god, and at the feast of penty-
cost by even porcions. And that all women that be or have byn sett
by or without the Churchwardens in any of the seates on the southe
syde Beinge Above the pulpett, Shall yerely paye vj d A pece At the
foresaid feastes by even porcions The same to be gathered by the
Churche Wardens or theire Assignes for the tyme beinge at theire
perell &c!³

Reading was across the Thames from the country home of Sir
Francis Knowles of Caversham, who was an important official in
Elizabeth's Council. His son, William, was a prominent member
of the parish of St. Laurence. "Unlawful" activity would be immediately noticed in Reading. More remote places were less likely
to conform. Elizabeth Baldwin suggests, in her essay, that the continuing activities in Cheshire were a deliberate challenge to the
authorities. Barbara Palmer uses many court documents recording
prosecutions to build her evidence for activities in the West Riding
of Yorkshire. She makes the helpful clarification that many activities were not considered unlawful in themselves, but because
they were being carried out on church property or in service time.
The town and parish of Newbury in Berkshire got round the
problem of using church property by holding the money raiser in
the guild hall.⁴

Different jurisdictions prosecuted the laws differently. Some
archdeacons regularly pressed the visitation questions about
church ales while others did not. In some areas of the country
such as Somerset and in some local situations such as the parish
of Windsor⁵ the continuation or suspension of the local customs
became a political flash point in local struggles between the religious conservatives and their more puritanical neighbours. Caution
must, therefore, be exercised in reading the evidence to place it in
its local context by considering such mitigating factors as the nature of the survival of the records, the proximity of the area to civil
or ecclesiastical seats of government and other factors of local significance. As the essays in this collection attest, although the

church ale was the fundamental event from which almost all parish activity grew, that activity was as varied and variable as the English countryside itself.

This collection is arranged to move from the consideration of the northern folk custom of rushbearing that survived well beyond our period to a consideration of two specific parish sponsored plays -- the Passion Play in New Romney, Kent, and the secular romance *Canimore and Lionley* performed by the parish of Methley, Yorkshire, in 1614. The arrangement is by no means chronological but meant to move from para-dramatic activities through the more hybrid and problematic events such as the king games and Robin Hood plays to what can be considered "true" drama with sets, props, texts and actors. The essays of David George and Elizabeth Baldwin on rushbearing are concerned with the records of Lancashire and Cheshire. Audrey Douglas' piece, after a general survey of parish dancing, concentrates on the activities in the Wiltshire cathedral town of Salisbury. Her discussion of ceremonial dancing has echoes in the customs of Ewelme and Wallingford in the Thames Valley.[6] James Stokes takes us farther west to Somerset where he discusses the custom of bear and bull baiting as that county's "entertainment of choice" to attract patrons to the church ales. Barbara Palmer returns us to the north, this time to the eastern side of the Pennines, and introduces the reader to the variety of parish entertainment in Yorkshire's West Riding including a discussion of a unique custom, the bearing of the Flower to the Well. Her essay is full of extensive citations from ecclesiastical court records that provide a rich sense of place and time. My own essay is based on the records from the upper Thames Valley and begins to turn the focus of the collection away from para-dramatic entertainments to actual plays, both secular and biblical. In it I suggest, as I have elsewhere more extensively[7], that Easter plays may be the most characteristic biblical play from which other episodic biblical drama was built.

The essays of Peter Greenfield using a broad spectrum of evidence from four counties adjacent to the Thames Valley and David Klausner using the single source of the journal of Prior More of Worcester both attest to the wide variety of parish plays south of the Trent/Severn divide. James Gibson's important reconstruction of the Passion Play in New Romney, Kent, provides a major new piece of evidence for the importance of Easter Drama. It also describes a play and a method of production strikingly similar to the Passion Play preserved in the *N-Town Plays*. Whether this shows that Kentish drama had affinities with East Anglian drama is impossible to determine. Nevertheless, the New Romney play adds another important middle sized biblical play to our consideration, standing between the major northern cycles based on salvation history and the smaller Easter plays from the parishes in the Thames Valley.

Finally, John Wasson's discussion of the secular romance performed in Methley adds one further dimension to the parish discussion. Although he expresses surprise at the choice of this play, there is later evidence from a Puritan pamphlet[8], that local thespians, like their twentieth century counterparts in parish halls all over the English speaking world, did mount "commercial" plays for the benefit of the parish coffers. The sad story of the parish players of Stanton Harcourt in Oxfordshire playing in the neighbouring town of Witney in 1652 attests to this practice. The Stanton Harcourt players mounted *Mucedorus*, a play performed in London over half a century before, for the expressed purpose of raising money for their parish. They toured it in the neighbourhood. We know of this because, during the performance in Witney, the floor of the pub where they were performing fell in, killing several people. This disaster proved to the local puritan who wrote the tract that divine retribution had overtaken the ungodly players and their hapless audience. Wasson's article ends with a discussion of how one of the four days of the performance of *Canimore and Lionley* coincided with the rushbearing to the church. This discussion nicely brings this collection full circle re-inforcing the fact that parish activity all over England -- for profit or communal celebration or both -- was varied and complex.

Notes

1   Alexandra F. Johnston and Margaret Rogerson [eds.], *Records of Early English Drama: York*, Toronto, University of Toronto Press, 1979.
2   Berkshire Record Office, D/A2/c. 40.
3   Berkshire Record Office, D/P 97 5/2 p. 349.
4   Berkshire Record Office, D/P 89 5/1.
5   Alexandra F. Johnston, "English Puritanism and Festive Custom", *Renaissance and Reformation*, 15 [NS] (1991), pp. 289-97.
6   Berkshire Record Office, W/ACa 1. fol. 55v.
7   Alexandra F. Johnston, "The Continental Connection: a Reconsideration", in Alan E. Knight [ed.], *The Stage as Mirror: Civic Theatre in Late Medieval Europe*, London, D. S. Brewer (forthcoming).
8   John Rowe, *Tragi-Comaedia*, Oxford, 1653.

Figure 1.
'A Lancashire Rush-Cart'. Undated; probably 19th century.
[From: Alfred Burton, *Rush-Bearing*, Manchester, 1891, p. 67.]

Rushbearing: A Forgotten British Custom

David George

No writer on early British customs should wait long to read Alfred Burton's *Rush-Bearing: An Account of the Old Custom of Strewing Rushes; Carrying Rushes to Church; The Rush-Cart; Garlands in Churches; Morris-Dancers; The Wakes; The Rush*, published in Manchester in 1891 and reprinted by Norwood Editions in 1974. This wonderfully undiscriminating book has lots of entries for rushbearing, and it proves that the ceremony was well-established and popular by Shakespeare's day. It remains, however, given the scarcity of the book, to re-explain the origins of the custom, its growth and its decline in the nineteenth century, and to add a few new observations garnered while I was collecting records for *Records of Early English Drama: Lancashire*, Toronto, University of Toronto Press, 1991.

Origins of the Custom
The custom seems to have begun with the cutting of rushes, commonly the *acorus calamus*, or sweet flag, 'not a rush at all [but] thus loosely classed by a rustic gatherer'.[1] Rushcutting, according to Burton, arose from the need to put something on the packed-earth floors of medieval houses. He quotes a payment in the Household Roll of Edward II (reigned 1307–27). One John de Carleford 'making a journey from York to Newcastle' was paid for a supply of rushes for strewing the king's chamber. In the fifteenth century, the Household Book of Edward IV records that the groom of the chamber was to bring daily 'rushes and litter for the paylettes all the year'. Many of the larger manor-houses had an officer called a 'rush-strewer' who had to see to it that daily rush-

es were brought in. Queen Elizabeth seems to have been the last English monarch to have her palace strewn with rushes.[2]

Not every noble or gentle house had the rushes changed daily. Burton comments: 'The straw and rushes were often allowed to accumulate in the houses until they became rotten and offensive, a fresh strewing serving to hide the filth beneath. ... An old author, writing in 1511, thus speaks of a custom which existed on "God's son-daye", or Easter Day: "Ye know well that it is the maner at this daye to do the fire out of the hall, and the black wynter brondes, and all things that is foule with fume and smoke shall be done awaye; and there the fire was shall be gayly arrayed with fayre flowres, and strewed with green ryshes all about." This process was termed "going to sweeten".'[3] The reader will observe that the replacement of rushes now has its own day. One might add here, by the way, that Burton claims that the open-air stages, such as the Globe, had rushes on them, so that we may have to contemplate stage battles being fought on a carpet of rushes.[4]

Growth of the Custom
Rushes were also used to cover the packed-earth floors of churches. At Kirkham, Lancashire, the church floor was rush-covered until 1634; at Saddleworth, it was rush-covered until 1826, when Bishop Law said some unkind things about it, and then the church floor was paved within a few years. Burton claims that 'the custom of taking these rushes to church gradually developed into a religious festival, and although some writers deny that there is any connection between the rushbearing and the wakes, or feast of the dedication of the church to some saint, the evidence is overwhelming that the custom of annually renewing the rushes did take place at that time'.[5] The overwhelming evidence is not conveniently given, nor is the key paragraph in the entire book immediately supported:

> As the wake was a religious festival, always commencing on Sunday, fresh rushes would be deemed necessary for the occasion. The getting of the rushes at such a time and bearing them to church would natu-

rally lead to some drinking and merrymaking; rivalry between the various townships in a parish would take place, and so the bundle of rushes would come to be decorated, the cart containing the rushes made ornamental, garlands of flowers obtained to decorate the church, till the rush-bearing at last became a picturesque spectacle.[6]

The use of that odd tense, the future perfect conditional (here obscured as the future conditional), warns us that we are dealing with a speculative tense. This speculation derives from one in the eighteenth century, which Burton quotes much later in his book:

In proportion as these festivals [the celebration of the birthday of the saint to which the parish church was dedicated] deviated from the original design of their institution, they became more popular, the conviviality was extended, and not only the inhabitants of the parish to which the church belonged were present at them, but they were joined by others from the neighbouring towns and parishes, who flocked together on these occasions, and the greater the reputation of the tutelar saint, the greater, generally, was the promiscuous assembly. The pedlars and hawkers attended to sell their wares, and so, by degrees, the religious wake was converted into a secular fair. Booths were erected, often in the churchyard, though this use of the churchyards had been frequently forbidden by Church councils, beginning from the time of Edward I.

Burton gives as authority for this passage 'Bourne "Antiq. Vulg.", 1777.'[7] This is very late evidence, unsatisfactory to students of Renaissance customs, yet there is no question but that rushbearing was some sort of church-sponsored ceremonial one hundred and fifty years before Bourne's observations. The following passages prove that:

23 October 1622: Robert Aughton of Penwortham was presented to the Visitation or Church Court as contumacious the -- charge, 'for not bearing Rushes with his towne to the churche.'

26 September 1623: John Bell, Henry Knowle, Henry Walker, and Richard Birches, churchwardens of Garstang, were summoned before the bishop at his Consistory Court in Chester -- the charge, 'having

warned the parishioners (under a penalty of ten groats a household) to bring rushes to the church on the Sunday, whereas St James' Day was the day of rushbearing appointed by the bishop.'[8]

Evidently the church wanted townspeople to bear rushes together, and to do it on a certain day. Church sponsorship is also indicated by items from early churchwardens' accounts showing that at rushbearings the church bells were rung (Chester, 1546–52), and that wine, sometimes with ale and cakes, for the rushbearers was paid for by the parish (Congleton 1595, 1599, 1607).[9]

The Rushcart
Burton was unable to demonstrate the use of a rushcart before 1726. This 1726 record, by a man named the Honorable H. Egerton, implies that the ceremonial rushcart he saw was of some long standing: 'As to ours of Prestwich, we have nothing but a Custom of bringing Rushes to Church in a cart, with great Ceremony, Dancing before it, and Cart and horses adorned with Plate, Ribbons and Garlands. The time anciently and usually observed is about St. Bartholomew's Day [25th August], whenever 'tis supposed its dedication is to yat Saint'.[10]

A rushcart for carrying a load of rushes to the church, while not attested in the Elizabethan and Jacobean period, could nevertheless easily have existed. Robert Herrick has a poem in *Hesperides* (published 1648), written between c. 1613 and 1648 and called 'The Hock-cart, or Harvest home'. 'Come forth, my Lord', writes Herrick to the Earl of Westmorland, 'and see the Cart / Drest up with all the Country Art. / ... About the Cart, heare, how the Rout / Of Rurall Younglings raise the shout / ... Some blesse the Cart; some kisse the sheaves; / Some prank them up with Oaken leaves' (ll. 7-8, 15-16, 19-20).[11] This hock-cart was presumably brought home to the manor-house in the late autumn, and the manner of its homecoming closely resembles the two pictures I have reproduced of Lancashire rushcarts, both done in the nineteenth century (Figures 1 and 3). The dancing in front of the cart is morris dancing, which is unlikely to have begun in the nineteenth century.

Perhaps Herrick's 'Hock-cart' is as close as we will get to the pre–1642 custom of bearing rushes to church, except for a suggestive passage in Raines' edition of *The Journal of Nicholas Assheton of Downham*, in which Raines remarks that the Whalley parish church accounts are extant for the years 1636 to 1700 and that they lack any reference to rushbearing. Then, after that, he adds, there are regular rushbearing entries *once more*; the date for the ceremony appears to be still St. James day, and there was a rushcart and garlands. This looks like a revival of the old custom. Raines notes that the rushcart disappeared about 1778, but that still in 1800 morris-dancers, booths, horse-races and rustic sports characterized the day.[12]

The rushcart may have disappeared at Whalley in about 1778, but according to Burton, in 1891, rushcarts were still used elsewhere in Lancashire though 'few men are now to be found who are able to build a rush-cart'.[13] Pictures of a Lancashire rushcart, in the nineteenth century, show that it was an elaborate affair, up to twenty feet high. A two-wheeled farm cart was piled high with rushes, carefully laid in haystack-fashion, the whole shaped like a bulging pyramid. Flowers decked the arcs over the wheels and branches of some flowering plant were stuck in the top. The rear of the stack was decorated with a coat of arms.[14] A horse or men, or both, pulled the wagon through town and to the parish church.[15]

Early Evidence of Rushbearings

While we may not get closer than Herrick's poem to early ceremonial rushbearing, it is rather easier to say what went wrong at rushbearings. Rushbearing was not permitted during divine service, and so the church called many into the ecclesiastical court over the violation of that order. In 1578, there were disturbances caused by rushbearers during divine service at Eccles and Woodplumpton parish churches. At a Whalley rushbearing in 1604 a piper played, a man danced and three men were accused of 'stry-vinge' about the rushes in the churchyard. More trouble occurred at Garstang in 1608, when three men rushed violently into the church at a rushbearing, having given the church officers some 'vndecente' words en route. Piping took place at a Goosnargh rushbearing on a Sunday in 1611. James I evidently decided that men should get out of the business of Sunday rushbearing, and gave leave to women only ('the women to have leave to Carrie rushes to ye Church for the decoringe of it accordinge to theire ould Custome') after the end of divine service in his 'Declaration Concerning Lawful Sports', intended for Lancashire when it was first written in late August 1617. A month before, on 25 July 1617, the ceremony had 'much less solemnitie than formerlie' at Whalley, according to Nicholas Assheton of Downham.[16]

Not all early allusions to rushbearing are negative, however. At Childwall parish church, the churchwardens' accounts are extant, and they show that money was spent in 1621–22, 1622–23 and 1625–56 for bringing rushes to the parish church from nearby villages. In 1622–23, the churchwardens spent 6d 'to see Rushes brought to the Church in decent manner, fro lytle Wolton'.[17] The main point to remember in favour of the propriety and popularity of rushbearing, however, is that when Sir Richard Hoghton had King James as a visitor at Hoghton Tower in 1617, he decided to make a rushbearing the first item of the royal entertainment on Sunday, 17 August. Nicholas Assheton comments: 'To dinner. About 4 o clock, ther was a rushbearing and pipeing afore them, affore the King in the middle court; then to supper'.[18] This is a very striking incident indeed, especially as the rushbearers proba-bly progressed into a part of the hall. The likelihood is that rush-bearers sometimes did bear rushes into buildings other than churches. It seems possible, too, that James was sufficiently im-pressed with Hoghton Tower's Sunday rushbearing to permit the practice after divine service was over.

Figure 2.
'Rush-Bearing'. Undated; probably intended to represent 18th-century rushbearing. [From: Alfred Burton, *Rush-Bearing*, Manchester, 1891, p. 26.]

Figure 3.
'Failsworth Rush-Bearing'. Undated; probably 19th century.
[From: Alfred Burton, *Rush-Bearing*, Manchester, 1891, p. 58.]

Allusions in Brathwait

That is all the evidence of rushbearing collected for the *Records of Early English Drama: Lancashire* volume, but Burton has more. He quotes Richard Brathwait's *Whimzies, or, a New Cast of Characters* (1631), in which Brathwait writes of 'A Zealous Brother' very satirically. 'He keeps a terrible quarter in his sinne-full *Synodalls*, and denounceth an heauie woe upon all *Wakes, Summerings*, and *Rush-bearings*: preferring that Act, whereby *Pipers* were made *rogues* by Act of Parliament, before any in all the *Acts* and *Monuments*'. Of 'A Pedler', the author says: 'A Countrey *Rush-bearing*, or Morrice *Pastorall*, is his *festivall*: if ever hee aspire to plum-porridge, that is the day. Here the Guga-girles gingle it with his neat nifles: while hee sculkes under a Booth, and showes his wit never till then, in admiring their follies. He ha's an obscene veine of *Ballatry*, which makes the Wenches of the Greene laugh; and this purchaseth him, upon better ac-quaintance, a posset or a Sillibub'. This is very informative: the rushbearing could be called a Morris Pastoral, and so the man who danced at Whalley in 1604 was probably a morris-dancer. If a pedlar could make it his festival, then obviously a rushbearing was a day-long affair. As for the 'Guga-girles', they were presu-mably girls who liked gaudy trifles, or gew-gaws; the pedlar's 'nifles' were his trifles. The girls who jingled it with the pedlar's nifles may well have been wearing morris-bells and dancing to the rushbearing. 'Ruffians' also turned up at rushbearings, and were apt to quarrel with the minstrel and break his drone (his bagpipe). Finally, Brathwait tells us that the rushbearing or 'May-morish' required a painter: one wife, desiring to play a trick on a would-be seducer, told him 'how her Husband (being an Excellent Painter, and such an One as not a Rush-bearing or May-morish in all that Parish could subsist without him) was to go a good way (as she pretended) stay a long time from home about setting forth of a Pageant'.[19] Presumably, then, the rushbearing procession had banners, booths, or some other devices that required painting.

Probably all of Brathwait's allusions to rushbearing relate to Westmorland, where he lived from 1610 until his death in 1673.

Related Activities

Morris-dancing, flower garlands, wine, ale, cakes, bell-ringing, banners, booths and rustic sports all seem, at one time or another, to have been part of rushbearings. Morris-dancing was certainly connected with Lancashire rushbearings in the early nineteenth century. As Burton comments, 'Some hundreds of young men could be seen every autumn in Lancashire dancing the morris. Rush-carts were then numerous, and nearly all had dancers accompanying them.'[20]

Along with the rushes and the dancing, there may have been garlands of flowers. In 1626 the Wilmslow, Cheshire, churchwardens paid 4s 6d for 'dressinge the greate Churche Garlande'.[21] Burton quotes Lysons' *Magna Britannia* (1810) for evidence that the garlands were hung up in the church, but Thomas Dunham Whitaker, commenting on Assheton's entry concerning the Whalley rushbearing of 25 July 1617, says the garlands were hung on the steeple. He adds that booths were erected in the churchyard, that morris dancers played their part, and that St. James was honored with various kinds of athletic sports, but it is not clear whether Whitaker was referring to Assheton's day or much later.[22]

All in all, rushbearing offers a promising avenue of research, though given the survival of rushbearing well into the nineteenth century only in Lancashire and adjacent counties, it may be that the best evidence for the pre–1642 ceremony is in. On the whole, I think, it is probably not. Perhaps as Records of Early English Drama editors become aware of this ceremony, the outlines of the carrying of rushes to church will be filled in. A good idea of rushbearing in the time of Elizabeth I and James I is possible if the necessary imagination is applied to Burton's pictures and accounts. A useful illustration to contemplate is 'Rush-Bearing' (Figure 2), which looks to be nineteenth-century and shows eighteenth-century women carrying rushes on their heads into a venerable church; and a useful account to accompany it is the undated one by Lucas, the Marton (Lancashire) schoolmaster. Lucas gives a generic account: After the rushes were cut, they were made into long bundles and bound up with ribbons, fine linen, flowers, or in some other decorative way. The young women of the village chosen to perform the ceremony that year took up the bundles and, carrying them erect, began the procession, attended by crowds and music, drums and bell-ringing. On arrival at the church, the rushbearers set their burdens down and stripped them of their flowers and decorations. Then they and the crowd returned to the village to eat, drink and dance about a maypole.[23]

That is no doubt a staid nineteenth-century account; the men and women of the Tudor and Stuart periods seem to have been much more uninhibited, drinking and dancing in the churchyard before carrying the rushes into the church. Hence the Archbishop of York and the Bishop of Chester forbade the practice of Sunday rushbearing, so regularly that it must have persisted. Many of their injunctions mention 'Minstrels, Morice dauncers, or others, at Rish-bearings' and even forbid dancing in the church. I have found that the York and Chester injunctions of 1571, 1577–78, 1581, 1604, 1607, 1617 and 1628–89 all mention rushbearing as an abuse of the Sabbath (before 1581, as an abuse of the time of divine service only) and put it on a par with such things as bull-baitings and bear-baitings.[24]

One audience member (Paul Thomas) who heard this paper read in its original form commented that he had seen rushbearings at Grasmere and Ambleside in Westmorland as recently as 1991, performed on Saturdays. A tractor pulled the rushcart. These are doubtless revivals of the custom as it was gentrified in the Lake District in the nineteenth century, first at Grasmere by William Wordsworth in 1827. Related refined rushbearings took place at Borrowdale in c. 1882, at Ambleside in 1885 and at Grasmere in 1888. The 1885 Ambleside rushbearing featured the singing of

'The Rushbearing Hymn', written about fifty years earlier by the Rev. Owen Lloyd, and the 1888 Grasmere one had the rushes borne in the form of Christian crosses.[25] The 1991 rushbearings, though doubtless de-Christianized, seem to have been intended to be picturesque and aimed at the tourist.

Notes

1   Alfred Burton, *Rush-Bearing: An Account of the Old Custom of Strewing Rushes; Carrying Rushes to Church; The Rush-Cart; Garlands in Churches; Morris-Dancers; The Wakes; The Rush*, Manchester, 1891 [1974²], p. 170.

2   Burton, *Rush-Bearing*, pp. 2-3.

3   Burton, *Rush-Bearing*, p. 7.

4   Burton, *Rush-Bearing*, p. 11.

5   Burton, *Rush-Bearing*, p. 14.

6   Burton, *Rush-Bearing*, p. 15.

7   "Bourne 'Antiq. Vulg.' 1777" is John Brand's *Observations on Popular Antiquities* (Newcastle, 1777). Brand reprinted Henry Bourne's *Antiquitates Vulgares* (Newcastle, 1725), adding his own "Observations" after each chapter. The material on church saints' day celebrations is chapter XXX, "Of the Country Wake" (pp. 296-99) and Brand's "Observations" on that chapter (pp. 299-302). Burton has changed the order of the Bourne-Brand account and erased the distinction between Southern and Northern saints' day practices. The passage here quoted relates to Southern county practices. Neither Bourne nor Brand, both Newcastle men, mentions rushbearing.

8   Burton, *Rush-Bearing*, pp. 16-17; David George [ed.], *Records of Early English Drama: Lancashire*, Toronto, University of Toronto Press, 1991, p. 23.

9   Burton, *Rush-Bearing*, pp. 18-19.

10 Burton, *Rush-Bearing*, pp. 62-63.

11 J. Max Patrick [ed.], *The Complete Poetry of Robert Herrick*, Garden City NY, 1963, p. 141.

12 F. R. Raines [ed.], *The Journal of Nicholas Assheton of Downham, in the County of Lancaster, Esq. for Part of the Year 1617, and Part of the Year Following*, Manchester, 1848 [Chetham Society, vol. 14], pp. 29-30.

13 Burton, *Rush-Bearing*, p. 24.

14 See Illustration entitled 'Rush-Cart' in Burton, *Rush-Bearing*, p. 70.

15 See Illustrations entitled 'A Bury Rush-Cart' and 'Failsworth Rush-Bearing' in Burton, *Rush-Bearing*, pp. 52 and 58. 'Failsworth Rush-Bearing' is reproduced here as Figure 3.
16 George, *REED: Lancashire*, pp. 18-19, 113, 98, 22, 24, 230, and 145.
17 George, *REED: Lancashire*, pp. 10-11.
18 George, *REED: Lancashire*, p. 146.
19 "A Zealous Brother", in Richard Brathwait, *Whimzies, or, a New Cast of Characters*, London, 1631, p. 197; "A Pedler", in *A CATER-CHARACTER, throwne out of a Boxe By an Experienc'd Gamester*, London, 1631, pp. 19-20; "A Ruffian", in Brathwait, *Whimzies*, p. 132; *Ar't a-sleepe Husband?*, London, 1640, p. 78.
20 Burton, *Rush-Bearing*, p. 117.
21 Burton, *Rush-Bearing*, p. 89.
22 Burton, *Rush-Bearing*, p. 90; Whitaker's quotation is from Robert Halley, *Lancashire: Its Puritanism and Nonconformity*, Manchester, 1869, vol. I, p. 212.
23 Burton, *Rush-Bearing*, p. 38.
24 George, *REED: Lancashire*, pp. 213-15.
25 Burton, *Rush-Bearing*, pp. 29-36.

Rushbearings and Maygames in the Diocese of Chester before 1642

Elizabeth Baldwin

The Diocese of Chester, established in 1541, included all of Lancashire and the Deanery of Richmond in Yorkshire. I have chosen to speak of the Diocese rather than the County of Chester in this article for two main reasons. Firstly, rushbearings generally came under ecclesiastical jurisdiction, which makes it appropriate to speak of them in diocesan terms. Secondly, because of the distribution of the surviving ecclesiastical documents, instances of rushbearing in Lancashire which were not included in the Lancashire volume of Records of Early English Drama have been found during the course of research for the Cheshire volume. It is therefore hoped that this article may be to some degree complementary to David George's article on Lancashire parishes and their rushbearings elsewhere in this volume.

Rushbearing was a feature of Cheshire parishes as well as Lancashire ones. Payments to the rushbearers occur regularly in the borough account books of Congleton from 1588 to 1635, and although the entries are short, they do give a good deal of information about the activities connected with rushbearings. The earliest payments are simply 'bestowed vpon the Rushbearers', with sums ranging from 1s to 3s 4d.[1] As early as 1592–93 the neighbouring village of Buglawton is mentioned in connection with the rushbearing, and it would seem that the 'rushbearing' was paraded around the neighbouring villages. Congleton was part of a large parish, and it may be that different villages took turns to provide the rushbearing. The 1592–93 payment is 'at the Rushbearynge for buglawton', and in 1617–18 there is a payment of 3s

10d 'paid to Marie Spencer widowe for meate & drinke bestowed vpon lawton people that brought a Rushbearinge'. Marie Spencer was paid 6s in 1622–23 'which was bestowed vpn Buglawton ffoalkes who broughte a Rushbearinge to our Chappell by consente of the Overseers'.[2] A payment of 2s 6d 'bestowed in Ale and bread vpon those that brought Rushes out of Buglawton at the Rushbearinge' in 1633–34 may indicate that the Buglawton people were bringing rushes to the Congleton rushbearing. The expense of 18d for gunpowder 'shott at Rushbeareinge and for two Cords that the Constables had use for' suggests that Congleton was more involved in the rushbearing that year than simply providing refreshment for the rushbearers. This seems to be borne out by the fact that the rushbearing expenses fall into two main categories. The first category, into which the Buglawton payments fall, is that of payments to rushbearers, or to those who provide food and drink to the rushbearers. These are the earliest and most frequent entries, and, in addition to those already quoted, occur in 1595–96, 1600–01, 1601–02, 1606–07, and 1616–17.[3] The other type of entry indicates a more active involvement in the entertainment on the part of the borough. In 1601–02 Roger Stopport was paid 10d for both 'drummynge before the Rushbearers & clensyng the pryson houses'. He was, with Hugh Chesphord, paid 6d in the following year, 1602–03, 'for plaing before the Rushbearers', so that it would seem that the payment for drumming was a small one. There was also a payment of 16d to Thomas Parnell in 1602–03, for 'gunpouder bestoued at the Rushbearyng'.[4] Gunpowder becomes a regular feature in the rushbearing payments after this, although the rushbearing payments themselves become less regular. Gunpowder was provided in 1604–05 (12d), 1606–07 (amount indeterminate because of manuscript damage), 1632–03 (2s 8d), 1633–04 (18d, with two cords), and 1634–05 (1s 6d).[5] Music was occasionally provided, usually in the form of drumming, as in the instances already quoted. A drummer was paid 2s in 1633–34 for drumming at both the rushbearing and the wakes. As well, in 1626–27, 3s was given to 'a pyper or musitioner who played before the Rushbearinge by consent of mr Maior and the overseers'.[6] This seems to have been a special occasion, as not only is it unique in the Congleton accounts, but it also is a relatively high payment among the rushbearing expenses.

On the whole, rushbearings in Cheshire were not viewed with as much distrust as they were in Lancashire. An order of 1612 for the entire county of Cheshire, setting forth 'His Ma*jes*ties pleasure concer*n*ing recreations on sondaies or hollidaies' specifically allows 'the weomen to have leave to carry rushes to the Churche, for the decoring of it, according to their old Custome'.[7] Most of the rushbearing payments for Cheshire occur in a fairly positive context, as at Congleton. Occasionally, however, there were problems, as in 1601 at Macclesfield, when 'Elyale*zr* Johnson' was presented at the ecclesiastical visitation 'for abvsinge the Churchwardens att a Rushbearinge at maxfeil and taking the flowers awaie'.[8] The ecclesiastical authorities had the thankless task of maintaining a balance between the two extremes of opinion regarding rushbearing, and it is over these differences of opinion that the rushbearings frequently get into the visitation or consistory court records.

A disturbance at a rushbearing in Burnley, Lancashire, in 1603, tells how

> The maid servan*tes* and women Children w*i*thin the said Chappell-ries and p*a*rishes namely w*i*thin the said Chapelrie of Burnley haue vsed & still doe vse vpon some sonday or holiday in the som*mer* tyme yerly to Carie and bringe burdens of Rushes into there m*a*sters ffathers mothers mistresses and dames seat*es* w*i*thin the said Churches and Chappells and namely w*i*thin the said Chapell of Burnley aforesaid and in the said seat*es* to strawe the said Rushes to sitt and kneele vpon in tyme of divine service.

When the women and children tried to ʰring their rushes to the chapel

the said Simon walmesley will*i*am Tailo*r* and Robe*rt*e lingard did
then and <.>here hinder them and keepe them backe from so doinge
and in verie deede did lay violent hand*es* vpon them beate them and
thruste them out of the said Chappell.[9]

The authorities were similarly protecting the rushbearers in
1621 at Chipping, Lancashire, when various individuals 'moste
violently pulled the rushes asunder and abused them very vyle-
ly'.[10] There was also assault committed in this case, and it would
appear that the associated violence, especially as it was on the
church premises, is the main concern of the authorities, rather than
any enthusiasm for the custom of rushbearing.

Rushbearing itself was specifically forbidden on certain occasions, as can be seen from the court proceedings held at Wiganin
July, 1626. Edmund Balshaw 'Encomium de Low Church' was
charged

ffor that he caused a Rushbearing to be made in that Chappell vpon
Sond<..> xviij° Iunij 1626 being form*er*ly ordered not to suffer yt
by meanes whereof there were many dronke and m<...> prophanc*i*on
of divine service etc[11]

The objection on this occasion would probably have been to the
date of the rushbearing, as the ecclesiastical authorities had decreed that rushbearings were allowable only on the feast of St.
James (25 July), rather than on the patronal festival of the church
as had been the custom before the Reformation.

Inevitably, rushbearings, like wakes, were considered to have
recusant associations. Wakes were more associated with disorderly behaviour than rushbearings were, but as the associations with
recusancy were more frequently made, the distinctions seem to
have blurred between what was appropriate for a rushbearing and
what was appropriate for a wake. In Bunbury in 1618, as well as
being presented by the High Constable for drunkenness, swearing,
bearbaiting at the wakes and resisting arrest, John Boland the

bearward was also presented for 'beating his bea[t]res at Bunbury at St Iames tyde at the Rushbearing there being never non before, contrary to the king*es* booke'.[12] That a bearbait took place at a rushbearing as well as at a wake was sufficiently unusual for the constable to comment specifically upon it. I have found no other instances of bearbaits at rushbearings, and this may be an unique case. It would seem that the desire to annoy the Puritans, as well as a fondness for bearbaiting, had more to do with this rushbearing than recusancy.

There are, however, rushbearings which do seem to have defiantly recusant overtones. An example from Lancashire best illustrates this. The date of the citation in the Visitation Book is 1633, and the specific inclusion of crucifixes on the rushbearing indicates recusant leanings, while the presence of so many people, some of them armed, may have been more defensive than celebratory:

> Officiu*m* d*omi*ni con*tra* inhabitantes de horneby for bearinge Rushes on the Saboath day & prophaneing the[ir] saboath w*i*th Morrice dances & greate fooleries their lord of Misrule, their Clownes Piclers like Giant*es* ougly shapes Crosses & Crucifixes vpon their Rushes Marching like warrio*r*s, long staues Pikes, shooteing w*i*th gun*n*s & Muskett*es*[13]

It should be noted, however, that the main participants were dismissed, in the following year, with a warning.

Maygames, of which I have found fewer recorded instances than rushbearings, were also on occasion associated with recusancy, and with wakes. For example, at Little Budworth in 1594, a long Star Chamber case between John Egerton and John and Hugh Starkey claims that the Starkeys had supported the constables in their decision to hold the wakes, being, as Mr. Egerton puts it 'greatly affected & supe*r*sticiously <..>clyned to the obse*r*vinge & kepinge of the same wakes & such other lyke vayne & abolished Trashe'.[14] One of the constables, Hugh Holbrook, was actively involved in 'disorderly activities' associated with the wakes:

> And vpon the tuesdaye after the said wake daye diu*erse* of the said Rouges and evyll disposed p*erso*ns having in their hand*es* greene boughes resembling Maygames came dauncing into the sayd towne of litle Budworthe w*i*th a drom*m*e before them and the sayde Constable following after them.[15]

Clearly the Little Budworth activity 'resembling Maygames' was in fact taking place in July, in connection with the wakes. Although references are not always specific as to whether the activities were maygames or not, there are occasions on which maygames take place in other months than May. In 1621, the curate of Wybunbury, George Nicholson, was charged in the Visitations

> for neglectinge readinge of prayers vpon Mundaie in Whitson weeke 1620 goeinge to an Ale in the afternoone to a May game soe that another Minister was procured to p*er*forme the duetyes of the Church[16]

Monday in Whitsun week fell on 5 June in 1621. Wybunbury had considerable problems with its clergy at this time, and the case against Mr. Nicholson is simply part of a longer dispute between the parishioners and the clergy.

Another set of July 'games' comes from Bunbury in 1620. These are not specifically identified as 'maygames' but there are similarities to the Little Budworth garlands and dancing. The document is worth quoting at some length:

> Instructions <....>rninge the gross misdemeano*u*rs of some vngodly perso<..> in the towneship of Bumbury gatheringe to<..> ther great multitud*es* of rude and disordered p<...>le on the Sabboth day and at other tymes; <...>trary to the express warrant of his Ma*j*esti<..> Iustices of Assise published before in the P<...>sh church of Bunbury for preventing and rep<...>ing of all such disordered meeting*es* & Assemblyes:

The first disordered Assembly was occasioned by Richard Codding-toun who was putt in womans apparell on the Sabboth day in Iulie last, by Elizabeth Symme and otheres, at her fatheres house (a disordered Alehouse) which Elizabeth Symme together with David Wilkinson (two persouns notoriously suspected of Adulterie) were thought to be the cheefe Authors both of attyringe the fore sayd Coddingtoun in womans apparell, and vsinge him as a messenger with a great trayne of rude people tumultuously gaddinge after him from thence to the Church hill to bringe a present of Cheryes to the sayd Elizabeth where shee sate as Ladye of the game readie to receive them.

...

The second tumultuous Assembly was Iulie 25, occasioned by Thomas Broocke & Thomas Manninge in womens apparell dansing like women after one Peacocke a fidler. And by William Arrowsmith and Richard Stubbs both of them in disguised apparell with naked swordes in theire handes daunsing with those that were in womens apparell, a great multitude of disordered and rude people gadding a longe after them

...

The third disordered & riotous Assembly was August 5 Thomas Symme and Margaret Bettely thelder cheife Authors of the same gathering together a greater multitude, by carrying about a great & large garland [for th] decked with flours ribbandes tinsell & scarfes for the making whereof money was gathered: & Richard Vernon a piper hired, & soe riotinge from on towneshipp to an other, men and women so promiscuously & lasiviously daunsed about Thomas Symme (as about a maypole) bearinge vpp the garland[17]

The date of the second 'Assembly' is suggestive, as 25 July was the date on which rushbearings were officially permitted. The activities of 25 July do not, however, resemble a rushbearing as much as do those of the third offence, that of 5 August. The collecting of money for the garland, and the carrying of it from township to township, may suggest a rushbearing. It should be remembered that Bunbury was also the place where a bearbait was added to the rushbearing in 1618, as has already been mentioned.

Some maygames did, of course, take place in May a -- deposition in the Consistory Court of Cheshire, dated 11 May 1621, claims that Robert Wythers was

> a piper a Common scoffer and Iester and hath often times disguysed himself and taken vpon him the person of a foole or Iester Carrieinge in his hand a bauble att May games or other times to move idle people to gaze and laugh at his foolery and hath [...ed] ˄ ⌈ lytle or non other meanes butt pipeinge to live on⌉[18]

Although there are relatively few clear mentions of maygames from Cheshire, examples such as those quoted above do provide useful information about what may have been involved in a maygame. The garlands and dancing at Little Budworth clearly reminded the deponent of maygames, and Robert Wyther's activities suggest that the presence of a fool with bauble was usual at a maygame. The cross-dressing and presentation of a gift of cherries to the 'Lady of the Game' at Bunbury suggest that some sort of mimetic activity was included, although this instance is not specifically referred to as a maygame. Indeed, the Bunbury activities could well have been associated with rushbearings rather than maygames, given the dates of the 'disorders'. However, considering the unconventional inclusion of a bearbait at the Bunbury rushbearing two years before the 1620 disórders, it would seem that a certain element of the population were including as many activities offensive to the authorities, and specifically to the Puritanical element in the church, at their rushbearing as they could. The vicar of Bunbury at that time was Henry Hinde, biographer of and brother-in-law to the Puritan John Bruen. Edmund Burghall, in his "Providence Improved" states, in reference to an incident in 1628 that Henry Hinde had frequently preached against bearbaiting at Bunbury, and the events of 1618 and 1620 could have been a reaction against an unsympathetic attitude on the part of the church authorities.[19] Whether the motives of such a reaction were recusant or not is unclear.

There were perhaps fewer problems relating to rushbearings within the county of Cheshire than Lancashire, which may reflect a greater concern with the recusant problem in Lancashire. The rushbearings at Congleton seem to have proceeded peacefully for a number of years. The fact that innovations such as bearbaits were introduced at Cheshire rushbearings, and that maygames and rushbearings seem to have been confused or combined, suggest less a recusant activity than a wish to annoy the authorities and enjoy forbidden activities. The Hornby rushbearing of 1633, for all its giants and gunpowder, still appears as very much a rush-bearing, while the Bunbury rushbearing of 1618 seems to be just an excuse for a bearbait. It is worth noting that Congleton had rushbearings with drummers and gunpowder in the 1630s without attracting any official disapproval.

Notes

1   Congleton, Borough Account Book I, fol. 6v (1588–89: 4s, but a com-bined expense with 'tallow'), fol. 16r (1590–91: 3s 4d), fol. 23r (1592–93: 3s 4d), and fol. 29r (1594–95: 12d).
2   Congleton, Borough Account Book I, fol. 165v and fol. 223v.
3   Congleton, Borough Account Book I, fol. 37r (1595–96), fol. 56v (1600–01), fol. 66r (1601–02), fol. 80r (1606–07); Congleton, Borough Account Book I, loose booklet, fol. 22v (1616–17); Congleton, Order Book, fol. 56v (1595–96), fol. 76r (1601–02).
4   Congleton, Order Book, fol. 76v (1601–02); Congleton, Borough Ac-count Book I, fol. 72v (1602–03).
5   Congleton, Order Book, fol. 85v (1604–05); Congleton, Borough Ac-count Book I, fol. 80r (1606–07), fol. 294r (1632–33), fol. 307r (1633–34), and fol. 324r (1634–35).
6   Congleton, Borough Account Book I, fol. 307v (1633–34), and fol. 249v (1626–27).
7   London, Public Record Office, CHES21/3, fol. 371r-v.
8   Chester, Cheshire Record Office, EDV 1/12b, fol. 95r.
9   Chester, Cheshire Record Office, EDC5 (1603)/4/60, fol. 1v.
10   Chester, Cheshire Record Office, Visitation Books, EDV 1/23, fols. 69v-70r.
11   Chester, Cheshire Record Office, EDA 3/2, fol. 1r, Proceedings of a court

held at Wigan before Bishop Bridgeman, 12 July 1626.

12 London, Public Record Office, Ches 24/114/4, Presentments of the High Constable of Eddisbury Hundred, 25 July 1618, single sheet. 'Contrary to the kinges booke' is written above the line.

13 York, Borthwick Institute, Visitation Book, V.1633/CB.2, fol. 160r, Sunday, 16 November 1633, Proceedings of a court held for Lonsdale Deanery in Lancaster Parish Church, before William Hasdall, LLD.

14 London, Public Record Office, STAC 7/2/24, mb 5, Bill of Complaint of Mr. John Egerton.

15 London, Public Record Office, STAC 7/2/24, mb 2d, Deposition of William Walker of Little Budworth, husbandman.

16 Chester, Cheshire Record Office, EDV 1/23, fol. 64r, 17 August 1621.

17 London, Public Record Office, CHES 24/115/4, single sheet, July-August, 1620.

18 Chester, Cheshire Record Office, EDC 5 (1621)/8, Norton, 11 May 1621, two sheets, unnumbered. It is not clear whether Norton is in fact one of the several Nortons in Cheshire or in Staffordshire, as there is a reference to it as being in the diocese of Coventry and Lichfield. However, this is only in connection with the parish of one of the witnesses, and the fact that the case was tried in the Cheshire Consistory Court would suggest that the offence was committed in Cheshire, or at least that the offendors were Cheshire men. The final words are inserted above the line.

19 London, British Library Additional MS 5851, fol. 52v.

'Owre Thanssynge Day':
Parish Dance and Procession in Salisbury*

Audrey Douglas

'TOMORROW SHALL BE MY DANCING DAY' -- so runs the opening line of a traditional carol, whose verses interweave scenes in the life of Christ with the imagery of true love and dance. Keyte and Parrot have recently suggested that behind the present text, the result of oral transmission or imperfect adaptation, lies an original that dates from before the Reformation. This surmise is borne out by evidence for Salisbury where the term, 'dancing day', itself is found in a parish context as early as the fifteenth century.[1] Details of this occasion, discussed below, afford a new perspective on the place of dance in popular practice and lore. The dancing day emerges both as a celebration sanctioned by the church -- in some instances securely tied to the annual or liturgical round of the parish -- and an event driven by the need to raise casual revenues to eke out parish income. As a customary occasion in the context of the local community or parish, the dancing day was probably widely familiar to the English population, at least in the southern part of the kingdom, until well after the Reformation.

The outline of the dancing day can be largely comprehended through a web of entries preserved in churchwardens' or other accounts. Dancing is indicated either where money gathered *by* dancers is included under receipts in churchwardens' accounts, or where payments *to* dancers from a particular church are itemized in a source external to the parish (as, for example, in the Cambridge college accounts noted below). In the latter circumstances there is always a question as to whether the payments in fact ended up in churchwardens' hands, unless of course the payments are confirmed in receipts. It is indeed probable that parish dancing originated in secular custom, primarily for the profit of the participants or perhaps the community, and that it was only gradually, or occasionally, taken over by particular parishes as a means of supplementing church income.[2] Certainly it may be assumed that where one patron or major contributor is documented, others existed who cannot now be traced -- from institutions whose records are no longer extant to onlookers who dispensed small coins to the dancers as they saw fit.

The research summarized here indicates that dancing as a parish occasion was in evidence from the fourteenth to the seventeenth centuries. The dancing was often customary or seasonal, but might also occur as an isolated event serving a special purpose. Hence parishioners in medieval Cambridge and Bristol customarily danced on church dedication days, whilst in 1452 dancers in Southwark participated in a patronal festival and, at the end of the fifteenth century, a Plymouth parish danced in aid of a building fund. Up to the early sixteenth century, the parish of Dunmow, in Essex, held celebrations several times a year with dancers, players and musicians.[3] In Salisbury, from the fifteenth to the seventeenth centuries, dancing took place in Whitsun week with, it seems, a separate 'dancing day' for each of the city's three parishes. In all these places, dance was organized on a parochial basis, minstrels or waits were sometimes in attendance, and young women had a role both in the dance itself and in the associated fund-raising.[4]

As already indicated, the primary object of the dance was the systematic gathering of money. This is evident from the churchwardens' accounts (from Bristol, Plymouth, Southwark, Dunmow and Salisbury) where 'dancing money' or an equivalent term frequently occurs as a standard heading or item of receipt. The 'dansynge money' accounted for by Dunmow's churchwardens flowed in from tours of the surrounding countryside, whereby players, minstrels and dancers took in as many as twenty-three different communities. In some parishes, the fact of appropriation to another institution meant that inbuilt patrons could be relied upon for donations to the dance. For instance, revenues from St. Thomas's church in Salisbury were assigned to the upkeep of the cathedral fabric; this meant that the rector acted as procurator for the cathedral, accounting for parish revenues but delivering the profits to the cathedral fabric masters. Until 1539, it was the latter who rewarded the dance at St. Thomas's. Similarly, in Cambridge, dancers at Great St. Mary's (appropriated to King's Hall in 1343) and Little St. Mary's (originally the college chapel of Peterhouse, or St. Peter's as it was first known) collected money from college patrons. Dancers from All Saints seem to have relied on neighbourly ties for regular donations from King's Hall, which lay immediately to the west of the parish church.[5]

The records for Salisbury refer simply to the 'dancing' or 'procession' day; there are also payments to dancers (*trepidantes*). Ideally, of course, we should ask two questions: first, what was the nature of the dance performed, and second, how did it relate to the procession that took place on the same day? In practice, the form that the evidence takes, offering only a minimal vocabulary for the dance itself, must influence the course of this investigation. I shall concentrate, therefore, on the history and context of the dance, where possible exploring various aspects of the questions posed above. Given the paucity of literature on the subject, it is hoped that the ensuing discussion will encourage researchers to examine local records with an eye to uncovering the role of parish dance in the light of the suggestions made here.[6]

The late medieval population of Salisbury (New Sarum, founded in 1222), numbering from six to eight thousand, was distributed among three parishes lying to the north and east of the cathedral of St. Mary the Virgin: St. Martin's, which was older than the city itself, St. Thomas's, of early thirteenth-century origin, and St. Edmund's, founded in 1269 (see Figure 4). Between 1477 and the early seventeenth century, each of these parishes at some point either records a 'dancing day' for Whitsun week or otherwise alludes to dance and/or procession. I shall look here at the evidence, for both dance and procession, at St. Edmund's and St. Thomas's, and for the dancing day itself in all three parishes.

The church of St. Edmund of Abingdon, in the northeast of the city, was served by a college of priests. The parish population included weavers and shoemakers, possibly metalworkers and, since the parish boundary bisected the marketplace, a number of the city's more prosperous inhabitants. Churchwardens' account rolls for St. Edmund's are extant from the mid-fifteenth century.[7]

St Edmund's accounts (and similarly St. Thomas's, examined below) reflect aspects of Salisbury's pre-Reformation liturgical custom, in particular, the celebration of Rogation week (sometimes with the feast of St. Mark), one day in Whitsun (or Pentecost) week, and the feast of Corpus Christi. Each of these occasions was marked by a procession, for which payments to banner bearers and/or bell ringers were normally recorded. At St. Edmund's, payments of this kind at Whitsun are entered for the Thursday in Whitsun week which, in the first half of the sixteenth century, is named as 'procession day'.[8] Other entries suggest that St. Edmund's Whit Thursday procession, confined to the parish in the fifteenth century, was by 1518 literally moving beyond the parish as the means of conveying a customary seasonal payment of 'smoke farthings' to the cathedral.[9] This is demonstrated in six accounts of certain date (1518–44) where sums for such customary payments are coupled with those for waits or minstrels who 'bring in the procession'. The most explicit is that for 1521 which records that 2s 9d for the traditional smoke farthings payment was given to the cathedral, 'owre lady <church>', and 6d to the waits 'to bring in owre <prosesyon> to owre Lady Churche'.[10]

Entries for 1483, however, and for 1518 show that Whit Thursday ('procession day') was also known as the 'dancing day'.[11] The apparently equivalent terms, 'procession day' and 'dancing day', afford no precise indication of the relationship (if any) between procession and dance. Whether during this overall period St. Edmund's parishioners were performing a dance independent of the procession, or whether the procession incorporated a customary dance or was itself a form of dance, cannot be conclusively documented.

In Europe of course -- France, Spain, the Netherlands, Belgium and elsewhere -- dance associated with procession is known to have occurred in many places at various times of the year. Of particular interest is Louis Backman's discussion of examples from the diocese of Liège, where dance and procession at Whitsun were common, with participants carrying crosses, relics and banners. In the twelfth century, these occasions seem to have signified 'gratitude of the baptized to the Papal power', while at the same time occasioning 'a sort of tax paid to the church'. An interesting parallel to the Salisbury situation is afforded in a two-day event, starting on Whit Tuesday, carried out by the citizens of Verviers, who processed to the church of St. Lambert in Liège where they performed a *tripudium*, described as a hopping movement or dance.[12]

The Whitsun processions staged by Verviers (from the city boundary of Liège to the church of St. Lambert) and by St. Edmund's, Salisbury (from the parish church to the cathedral) share certain characteristics. The idea of tribute, for instance, is present on both occasions: St. Edmund's acknowledges the cathedral as mother-church, while the mayor of Verviers makes a speech declaring the inhabitants' age-old obligation to the church of St. Lambert; St. Edmund's parishioners present their small money payment, Verviers presents a purse containing token coins. A reciprocal gift is made or implicit in the ceremonial context: for St. Edmund's, episcopal and papal protection; for Verviers, similar protection, perhaps, symbolized in a gift of incense to the citizens from the clergy of St. Lambert. There may well be, in fact, an ecclesiastical tie of obligation underlying the latter procession, mingled with and obscured by other circumstances adduced by historians to explain its existence.

Figure 4
'Ancient View of Salisbury', showing, from left to right, St. Martin's, the
Cathedral, the Cathedral belfry, St. Thomas's and St. Edmund's.

[From: Peter Hall, *Picturesque Memorials of Salisbury*,
Salisbury, W. B. Brodie, 1834, plate I.]

For St. Edmund's we have only the descriptive and equivalent terms, 'dancing day' and 'procession day', on which to base any conjecture as to the actual role of dance in the Whit Thursday processions. It is notable, however, that references to dance in the parish record occur in the later sixteenth century, long after the Whitsun processions had ceased. Receipts entered under 'Dancing Money' in the churchwardens' accounts for various years in the period 1567–81 point to dance primarily as a means of parish fund-raising: on two such occasions bell ringers were paid, once for 'the Whitsun dance', and once in connection with the 'dancing day'.[13]

At this point it is necessary to refer to Salisbury's second oldest parish, St. Thomas's, whose more extensive records help fill in, though not complete, the picture of Whitsun dance in Salisbury up to the early part of the seventeenth century. The church of St. Thomas lay on the main route that ran from the north of the city southwards to the cathedral; Salisbury's market centre developed adjacent to St. Thomas's church where the tailors, pre-eminent among the city's crafts, had their chapel. Income from the church was the most important asset held by the cathedral dean and chapter's fabric fund, to which the parish was permanently appropriated in 1399.[14] Until 1539, at least, St. Thomas's accounts were kept by a cathedral chapter member acting as procurator; the profits he accounted for were in turn the subject of accounts kept by the chapter's masters of the fabric. At some time after 1539, however, the parish began to lease the rectory from the chapter, electing its own churchwardens to keep the accounts.[15]

Turning first to the thirty extant procurator's accounts, we find that St. Thomas's procession takes place on the Friday of Whitsun week, named not as the dancing day, but as the apparently synonymous 'Frick' Friday.[16] On this day there are payments for 'priests in procession in the church of St Thomas the martyr' in sixteen accounts from 1487 to 1514.[17] Thereafter no procurator's accounts of certain date either record such payments, or (in contrast to St. Edmund's accounts at this period) make any reference to smoke farthings. Clearly, St. Thomas's first Whitsun procession was a local event confined to the parish. Later though, between 1547 and 1600, sums for smoke farthing payments on Frick Friday are frequently mentioned in St. Thomas's churchwardens' accounts; at the same time, payments made for the Whitsun procession in 1547, 1557 and 1559 suggest that it had become the means of delivering smoke farthings to the cathedral.[18] So far, then, we have a situation comparable to that examined above for St. Edmund's: in each case the parish dancing day features a Whitsun procession which, while local at first, subsequently became the formal means of delivery of customary payments to the cathedral as mother church.

At St. Thomas's, however, important additional evidence exists for a customary Whitsun dance performed by parishioners on the day of the procession. Payments to dancers (*trepidantes*) on Frick Friday occur in the twenty-three extant accounts of the masters of the fabric (1477–1538). Four groups are singled out: variously described, they comprised married women, young female servants, daughters, and scholars or boys.[19] The antiquity of the dance is indicated by the use of the term, 'Frick Friday' (see note 16) and almost certainly the dance goes back well beyond the first recorded payment of 1478. Longstanding tradition is also implied in the fixed nature of the rewards given to each group of participants: married women received 6s 8d, servants 3s 4d, girls 20d and boys 12d. Customary refreshments dispensed at the event comprised bread and ale, cakes, confectionery (including dragées and comfits), and wine (red wine, claret, malmsey and rumney).

As Backman points out, the popular character of a dance such as this merges into the sacral, for the occasion may be sanctioned or even promoted by the church, with clergy appointing the dancers and attending the performance.[20] At St. Thomas's the rector, a member of the cathedral chapter, presided over the event, dispensing on the chapter's behalf (out of revenue appropriated to the cathedral fabric) cash rewards and money for the dancers' refreshments.[21] Dictated by custom, perhaps, the sums disbursed on food and drink varied only slightly from year to year, so that it is impossible to determine any fluctuation in the numbers participating.

Even though the unchanging level of cash rewards may suggest a fixed number of participants, there is no express indication of the rector's engaging the dancers and thus making of the dance a set piece rather than a community event. The composition of the first three groups of participants, named as married women (for which we may also read 'mothers'), daughters and young maidservants, points rather to a gathering of members of local households, flexible in number. The implication is that the dancers, rather than being hand-picked, turned up of their own volition to take part in a traditional spring celebration. The scholars or boys who joined the predominantly female dance were presumably the young sons of the households. Subsequent Whitsun gatherings in the period 1545–59 (see note 25) comprised daughters, sons and servants, pointing to the continuation of the household context suggested for the earlier *trepidantes*.[22]

For the female trepidantes, the dance meant perhaps escape from convention into a momentary freedom denied them in normal circumstances, more especially since dance was an activity often condemned by the very authority (the church) that was in this case overseeing it.[23] This is not to say that for the participants all constraints were removed. Dancing as a community act may imply the temporary lowering of customary barriers; but the categorical description of the Frick Friday participants and the scale of cash rewards all unvarying over the recorded period of sixty years suggest that status was traditionally maintained within the group. (Similarly suggestive is the range of food and drink dispensed on each occasion did the boys make do with bread and ale, for instance, while the older women indulged in wine and cakes?) The denomination of groups in the record also indicates that divisions between sex and age were maintained even within the dance itself.

It should also be stressed that money for *trepidantes* is found not as an item of receipt in the procurators' accounts (the precursor to St. Thomas's churchwardens' accounts) but as payments to the dancers recorded in the accounts of the cathedral fabric masters who patronized the event. Similarly, the occurrence of dancing in Cambridge parishes is known only through payments made by college patrons, or institutions to whom such parishes were appropriated (see note 5). The fact then that no references to *trepidantes* are extant for St. Edmund's parish, for which we have only churchwardens' accounts, does not rule out the possibility that up to the early sixteenth century *trepidantes* performed on St. Edmund's dancing day (Whit Thursday) in an event whose profits, as at St. Thomas's, left no trace as a *receipted* item of parish revenue.

The reasons for this lacuna may be sought perhaps in the changing circumstances of Salisbury's Whitsun dance itself. In the case of St. Thomas's *trepidantes*, it is likely that the total sum of rewards (12s 8d) was swelled by other solicited contributions. What happened to the money? As noted above, up to the early sixteenth century other parishes accounted for dancing money as itemized revenue; in Salisbury, receipts for Whitsun money are not found at either St. Edmund's or St. Thomas's until the middle years of the sixteenth century. A clue is provided in the circumstances at St. Thomas's. First, with the leasing of the rectory some time after 1539, the parish vestry itself became responsible for income and expenditure, with churchwardens appointed to keep the accounts. Second, money gathered at Whitsun now begins to appear as an item of receipt, at first in conjunction with income at Hocktide. The combination of these sources of revenue in the accounts suggests a deliberate take over of customary local practices. Profits formerly raised in a secular context and spent as the participants saw fit on themselves, on a wider community celebration, or on ad hoc church projects were now routinely diverted to church purposes and recorded by churchwardens as regular income. Both Hocktide and Whitsun, in fact, were seen as providing opportunities for money gathering in which various groups of parishioners could, and were probably expected to, participate. In St. Thomas's case, the decision may be linked to the new administration (the vestry). St. Edmund's, which by this time had already appropriated Hocktide profits, only starts to account for Whitsun dancing money some twenty years later, in 1567.[24]

The nature of the early Whitsun gatherings at St. Thomas's is not immediately evident. The wording of the accounts, however, suggests that to begin with there was a split between Hocktide and Whitsun gatherings based on age, if not generation. From 1545 to 1561, Hocktide is referred to in terms of men and women; Whitsun in the period 1545–59 is generally referred to in terms of the young, that is, as daughters, sons, or servants these are in fact three of the four groups named as *trepidantes* in the fabric masters' accounts of the earlier period. While not conclusive, this evidence, together with allusions to Whitsun dance in the parish in the latter part of the sixteenth century (see notes 27-28), suggests that the interim mid-century gatherings formed part of a continuum of Whitsun gatherings, all focused on dance, but now with only the young (male and female) participating. The celebration of Hocktide,however, as a men's and women's event (where presumably older adults were welcome) continues with gaps until 1570.[25] In 1571 there is a significant change: for the next nine years, we find mention only of 'women's and maidens'' gatherings at both Hocktide and Whitsun.[26] Gender rather than age now determines responsibility for active fund-raising: women and girls participate, men and boys do not.

Overlapping these years are the first specific references in St. Thomas's accounts to a children's dance at Whitsun (1577–79), with payments to the church sexton who 'guided' the dance.[27] Originating as a separate event, it eventually superseded the gatherings of women and girls; after a gap of thirteen years, Whitsun entries resume with allusions only to the children's dance, ending in 1599. The chance survival of an account book (rather than account roll) for 1598 shows that minstrels and bell ringers were also paid in connection with the dance. The last mention in St. Thomas's churchwardens' accounts of children gathering money (not specifically linked with dance) occurs for 1601. Sporadic gatherings at Whitsun continue, sometimes with no sums entered; the final sum is for 1620, although the Whitsun subtitle remains in the record until the account for 1623–24.[28]

Whitsun dancing as a source of casual revenue is also found in the churchwardens' accounts of Salisbury's oldest parish, St. Martin's. Accounts are extant only from 1567 so that there is no evidence, from this source at least, for the Whitsun processions found in the other two parishes in the earlier half of the sixteenth century. Comparable entries, however, for dance, dancers or gatherings are found in St. Martin's accounts from 1568 to 1624; it is tempting to speculate that the parish dancing day was Whit Wednesday, in which case the three parishes would have had their dancing days in succession.[29]

The end of Salisbury's dancing days apparently coincides with a justices' order promulgated on 5 April 1624. Its substance, banning Whitsun dancing from the cathedral and its cloister during services, points to the continuation of Whitsun dance even after specific mention in Salisbury's parish accounts disappears.[30] Incidentally, not only did the three city parishes dance through Salisbury to the cathedral and its close (perhaps successively, Wednesday to Friday) but the inhabitants of Wishford and Barford, communities some two miles outside the city, also danced into the cathedral on Whit Tuesday to claim before the altar their customary rights in the forest of Groveley. Four days in Salisbury's Whitsun week, therefore, may sometimes have been marked by dancing, with money gathered on at least three of these occasions. A customary Whitsun fair, held in the cathedral close on Monday, Tuesday and Wednesday must have compounded the revelry and congestion.[31] Little wonder that cathedral services were under strain!

To sum up so far: from the later fifteenth century, both St. Edmund's and St. Thomas's name a dancing day, also known at St. Edmund's as the procession day; the two parishes respectively observed Whit Thursday and Whit (Frick) Friday. Each dancing day coincided with a customary parochial Whitsun procession; in both parishes the procession appears at some time in the sixteenth century (up to the early years of Elizabeth I) to have become a means of delivering customary Whitsun smoke farthing payments to the cathedral. At St. Thomas's, four groups of *trepidantes* were rewarded with money and refreshments on Frick Friday, an occasion evidently of some antiquity. From the middle years of the sixteenth century, both parishes, together with St. Martin's, show evidence of dance, now patently a fund raising event. At St. Thomas's, the children's dance, mentioned in the last twenty or so years of the century, was possibly derived from a dance performed at the earlier mid-sixteenth-century Whitsun gatherings, first of younger people, both male and female, then of women and girls.

Finally, on the basis of this review, we may look at one further possibility: that the interchangeable 'Frick Friday/dancing day/ procession day' usage reflects the interdependence of dance and procession in Salisbury's Whitsun week -- that is, the dance accompanied or was incorporated into the procession, and hence could be considered to have a liturgical association itself. Two points may be made here. First, waits were employed by St. Edmund's church to bring its Whitsun procession into the cathedral (see note 10). While music does not necessarily imply dance, this fact in conjunction with other evidence may be significant. In fact, the whole question of the ritual surrounding the 'bringing in' of a procession is pertinent here. For instance, St. Edmund's also made various payments, from 1538 to 1556, in connection with candles that were brought into the church on 2 February (the Purification of the Blessed Virgin Mary) on behalf of the 'wives'. On several of these occasions there is reference to a wives' dance, sometimes in conjunction with a payment to minstrels or waits.[32] Are we looking here at a form of processional dance performed by

53

the women to accompany the entry of their light into the parish church on the feast of the Purification another dancing day in fact? If so, then perhaps something similar may be hypothesized for the bringing in of the Whitsun processions in Salisbury, whether to the parish church itself, or to the cathedral.

The second point to be made is that the children's dance (1577–79), guided by the sexton, and the justices' order of 1624, banning dancers from entering the cathedral or cloister, both provide evidence that the later sixteenth-century Whitsun dance was processional or at least perambulatory in character. The substance of the justices' order also reveals that the route took in the cathedral. The Whitsun processions of St. Edmund and St. Thomas, as noted above, took customary payments of smoke farthings to the cathedral as mother church. It is significant, then, that the seventeenth-century Whitsun dance had the same destination as the old processions, long after these were abandoned.

Again, as with so much of this material, no firm conclusion can be drawn. The suggestion is strong, however, that the Whitsun dance, in following the old processional route to the cathedral, had once been closely associated with the procession itself. Originally, perhaps, a number of parishioners, or several customary groups, such as those that made up St. Thomas's *trepidantes*, danced in or with the procession, bringing it into the parish church, while their successors, the women, girls and boys of the early Whitsun gatherings (1545–59), brought the smoke farthings procession into the cathedral. At the same time, as we have seen, possibly from 1545 (St Thomas's), and certainly from 1568 (St Edmund's and St. Martin's), it was customary at Whitsun for parishioners to gather money for their church in some form of dance; this practice may well derive from a deliberate take-over of secular custom for the profit of the church. After the Whitsun processions ceased in the early years of Elizabeth's reign the gathering of money remained as the principal purpose of the dance.

The last years of the sixteenth century in Salisbury were marked by a deepening economic depression, whose effects dogged the city well into the latter part of the seventeenth century.[33] It may be assumed that industrial dislocation, plague or its threatened outbreak, dearth, poverty and unemployment, together with the sometimes repressive remedies undertaken by the city, played a variable but always discouraging role with regard to the Whitsun dance, principally, in severely thinning the ranks of participants, in weakening the community obligations and resolve of those parishioners who survived infection, and in lessening the number of onlookers in the streets able or willing to give handouts to the dancers. Even those who escaped plague or poverty contributed to municipal relief schemes and were less likely to part with their money, as they had done in the past, in response to merely customary demand. The vestry of St. Martin's, perhaps the poorest of the city's parishes, decided c. 1598–99 to devote Whitsun income to the placing of a poor apprentice with a master.[34] This act, while it may reflect increasing Puritan unease with the dance itself, also coincides with the implementation of a municipal policy that stressed, among its various measures, the setting to work of the poor. After an apparent hiatus of twenty-six years, St. Edmund's Whitsun dance was briefly revived (1608, 1609, 1611), perhaps to meet urgent needs.[35] As the richest of the three parishes, St. Thomas's contributed to relief in St. Edmund's and St. Martin's. Nevertheless, in St. Thomas's churchwardens' accounts, fluctuating amounts gathered at Whitsun, and occasional sums left blank or 'not gathered', suggest an overall decline in the parish dance in the seventeenth century both in terms of income and of incidence.[36]

By the 1620s, a predominantly Puritan municipal administration found itself dealing with a sizeable proportion of the population that was poor, out-of-work or vagrant. Under these circumstances the end of the dancing day was spelled out, it seems, not in economic or religious terms, but in an administrative order that may well have been aimed at the unruliness of the event. The Whitsun dance had long been removed from its original and valid context, where, as a parish and possibly para-liturgical event, it had its proper root. Authorities in the city and in the cathedral close, where immigrant unemployed and beggars congregated, discovered that poverty constituted a problem of policing as much as relief any assembly of citizens, in hard times, might lead to disturbance.[37] The justices' order apparently recognized this threat in the Whitsun dance, now solely a means of fund-raising, a begging procession conducive to unruliness and disorder. In banning access to the cathedral, the traditional destination of the old Whitsun procession, the justices signalled the demise of the dance, severing its last link with its origin as a customary event in the pre-Reformation church's liturgical calendar, and delivering the unspoken sentence that it had become not only irrelevant but a nuisance. For Salisbury's dancing days there would be no more tomorrows.

Notes

*   This article was first published in *Folk Music Journal* 6 (1994), pp. 600-15, and is reprinted here by kind permission of the editor. Subsequent to its preparation, a British Academy personal research grant has facilitated the sorting and renumbering of a large portion of the fragmented churchwardens' accounts for St. Edmund's, Salisbury, described in note 7, below.

1   'Tomorrow Shall Be my Dancing Day', Hugh Keyte and Andrew Parrot [eds.], *The New Oxford Book of Carols*, Oxford, Oxford University Press, 1992, pp. 464-66 and 467 (note); for Salisbury usage, see notes 11 and 16 below.

2   Cfr. Hocktide custom, note 24 below.

3   Alan H. Nelson [ed.], *Records of Early English Drama* [hereafter *REED*]: *Cambridge*, 2 vols, Toronto, University of Toronto Press, 1989, vol. II, pp. 734-35: dedication days -- All Saints (1 November, 1398–99 to 1420–21), Great St. Mary's (variously mid-May to early July, 1342–43 to 1477–78) and Little St. Mary's (11 July, 1405–06 to 1472–73); Bristol Record Office, P/StE/ChW/1, St. Ewen's, churchwardens' accounts, fols. 27r, 49v, 58r: entries for 'daunsyng mony', 1455–56, 1464–65 (dedication day), 1467–68 (my thanks for this citation to Mark

Pilkinton, research editor, *REED: Bristol* [forthcoming]); Greater London Record Office, P92/SAV/1, St. Margaret's, Southwark, churchwardens' accounts, p. 7: St. Margaret's Day, 1452, 'recuyd in dawnsyng mony of the maydens iij s iiij d', with associated entries for players, minstrels and procession (my thanks to Sally-Beth MacLean, research editor, *REED: Surrey* [forthcoming]; John M. Wasson [ed.], *REED: Devon*, Toronto, University of Toronto Press, 1986, p. 214: St. Andrew's, Plymouth, churchwardens' accounts, 19 February 1499–1500, memorandum itemizing receipts and debts for 'dawnsyng mony', contributed to a new steeple; J. R. Smith, "The Suppression of 'Pestiferous Dancing' in Essex", *English Dance and Song* 3 (1974), n° 1 (Spring), p. 9: Dunmow parish, churchwardens' accounts, receipts and expenses for dancing at Christmas, Plough feast (early January), May Day, 'the games of the bishop of St. Andrew' and Corpus Christi. The term, 'dancing day', found in Salisbury, is not in these accounts; dance as a church money-raising activity, however, the chief concern of the event in Salisbury, is a common characteristic of all the examples cited here, a fact that implies familiarity with the dancing day as a routine and well-understood occasion.

4   Nelson, *REED: Cambridge*, vol. II, p. 735, minstrels/waits; MacLean, *REED: Surrey*, minstrels; Nelson, *REED: Cambridge*, maidens/puellae dancing; Salisbury (see note 19 below), women, girls and maidservants dancing; Pilkinton, *REED: Bristol*, pp. 8-9, Wasson, *REED: Devon*, p. 214, and MacLean, *REED: Surrey*, women accounting for dancing money.

5   Smith, "Suppression", p. 9; Salisbury, note 21 below; Nelson, *REED: Cambridge*, vol. II, pp. 734-35.

6   My research for Salisbury has been supported by funding from *Records of Early English Drama* through a negotiated grant from the Social Sciences and Humanities Research Council of Canada, and by a subsequent grant from the same body. The present article is based on a paper given at the 7th Triennial Colloquium, Société Internationale pour l'Etude du Théâtre Médiéval, Girona, 1992. My grateful thanks are due to the staff of the Wiltshire Record Office, Trowbridge, and to Suzane Eward of the Dean and Chapter Archive, Salisbury, where the research was carried out.

7   Victoria County History [VCH], *Wiltshire*, London, Oxford University Press, 1962, vol. VI, pp. 83-85, 151-53; Alison Borthwick and John Chandler, *Our Chequered Past*, Trowbridge, Wiltshire Library and Museum Service Trowbridge, 1984, p. 61. Wiltshire Record Office [hereafter WRO] 1901/66-77, St. Edmund, Churchwardens' Accounts 1443–1603 with gaps [hereafter SEA 1-12]; bundled fragments (unnumbered) in

twelve lots, with minimal ascription; reference also to the transcription (sometimes abridged) in Henry Swayne [ed.], *Churchwardens' Accounts of S. Edmund and S. Thomas, Sarum 1443–1702*, Salisbury, Wiltshire Record Society, 1896 [hereafter CWA].

8   Whit Thursday, under 'Expense' -- SEA1 1461–62, 1462–63, 1469–70 (CWA, pp. 8, 9, and 13); 'Custus' -- SEA2 1482-83 (CWA, p. 29); Payments' -- SEA4 1527–28, 1533–34, 1538–39 (CWA, pp. 68 and 70 [wrongly dated 1532–33], 84); 'Solutions' -- SEA7 1556–57, 1557–58 (CWA, pp. 101 and 103). Procession day, 'Solutions' -- SEA3 *recte* 1542–43 (CWA, p. 63); SEA5 1541–42 (CWA, p. 87); SEA4 1543–44 (CWA, p. 88). (All Salisbury churchwardens' accounts have their term at or near Easter, Whitsun thus falling within the first year of each account period.)

9   Variously described as a hearth-tax, pentecostal's or Peter's pence, the smoke farthing payment was defined in 1710 as 'customary oblations offered by the inhabitants of a diocese when they made their procession to the mother or cathedral church' (*Oxford English Dictionary*, Oxford, Oxford University Press, 1989^2, vol. XV, p. 803).

10 < > indicates reading inferred from a defective manuscript. Under 'Banner bearers' -- SEA4 1521–22 (CWA, p. 65, entries abridged); also 'Laid out' -- SEA4 1518–19 (CWA, p. 64); SEA5 1536–37 (no heading offering recorded for 'whitsunday' perhaps in error; not in CWA); 'Payments' -- SEA4 1538–39 (CWA, pp. 83-84); 'Solutions' -- SEA4 1540–41, SEA4 1543–44 (CWA, pp. 86 and 88); also SEA7 1557–58 (CWA, p. 103), where the brief restoration of the Catholic church is reflected in sums for smoke farthings, waits, 'waring of the copes the thursday in the whitsonweke' and 'Syngers and minstrelles'.

11 Collation of Latin and English versions of 1483–44 account: under 'Custus' -- SEA2 (CWA, p. 31), banner bearing, ringing for the procession 'in quinta fferia Septimane pentacosten'; 'Costs' -- SEA5 (CWA, p. 33), banner bearers, bell ringers 'vn owre thanssynge Day'. Also 'Laid out' -- SEA4 1518–19 (CWA, p. 64), bell ringers on 'dawnsynge day'.

12 The *tripudium* also characterized the Whitsun dance in Echternach, Luxemburg, enacted up to the present century; Louis E. Backman, *Religious Dances in the Christian Church and in Popular Medicine*, trans. by E. Classen, London, Allen and Unwin, 1952, pp. 85, 116, 117 (a detailed chronological study from the foundation of the Church to the nineteenth century). While specific circumstances are adduced to explain the Verviers dance, Backman suggests that its rich and colourful details originated in rituals for the prevention of famine and the promotion of fertility (p. 115). See also Dom Louis Gougaud, "La Danse dans les Eglises", *Revue*

d'Histoire Ecclésiastique 15 (1914), pp. 3-22 and 15 (1914), pp. 222-45, for a wide survey of Europe to recent times; and J.G. Davies, *Liturgical Dance: An Historical, Theological and Practical Handbook*, London, SCM Press, 1984, pp. 49-54, summarizing chiefly European evidence from 1200 to 1500.

13 Dancing money: SEA8 1567–68 (CWA, p. 110); SEA9 1572–73 (CWA, p. 119); SEA12 1573–74, wrongly labelled as c. 1575–80 (CWA, p. 118); SEA12 1577–78 (labelled as c. Elizabeth I -- not in CWA); SEA10 1581–82 (CWA, p. 131); eight other contemporary entries (seven of uncertain date) include: under 'Repair of Church Lytton', SEA9, wrongly labelled c. 1570 (CWA, p. 128 1575–76), bell ringers, Whitsun dance; and SEA9, fragment labelled c. 1570s (CWA, p. 126, probably after 1579), bell ringers, dancing day.

14 VCH, *Wiltshire*, vol. VI, pp. 81, 147-48; after 1537, the church, originally dedicated to Thomas Becket, was known as St. Thomas the Apostle.

15 Salisbury Cathedral Archives, St. Thomas: Press 2, Box 1, 1486–1514 [hereafter STP1-15]; Box 2, 1520–39 [hereafter STP16-27]; twenty-seven Procurators' Accounts, some incomplete, fourteen of uncertain date; end dates given here are from accounts of certain date; Press 2, twenty-three Accounts of the Masters of the Fabric on Receipts of St. Thomas 1477–1538 [hereafter STF1-23]. WRO, St. Thomas: 1900/65-7, three Procurator's Accounts (labelled in error as Churchwardens' Accounts) dated 1488–89, c. 1516–21, 1490–91 [STA1a-c] -- STP and STF accounts run from Michaelmas, Whitsun being in the second year of each accounting period; 1900/68-79 and 81, Churchwardens' Accounts 1546–1626 in thirteen lots, with gaps [hereafter STA2-13 and 16].

16 *Frick*, with a recent dialect meaning, 'to move briskly', is related to Anglo-Saxon *frician*, 'to move briskly or dance' (Joseph Wright [ed.], *The English Dialect Dictionary*, London, Henry Frowde, 1900, vol. II, p. 496). Wright does not make the connection with *frig* (now a vernacular term for copulation), though its original sense, like that of *frick*, is 'to move about' (*Concise Oxford English Dictionary*, Oxford, Oxford University Press, 1982[7], p 394). The term may point to a pre-Christian origin for the dance.

17 STP1 1486–87; STA1c 1490–91; STP3 c. 1489–95; STP2 1493–94; STP4 1495–96; STP5 1499–1500; STP6-9 1504–08; STP12 c. 1508–11; STP10 ?1508–09; STP11 1509–10; STP13 1511–12; STP14 ?1512–13 STP15 1513–14; also STP16-17 n.d.

18 Payments for Frick Friday under 'Allocations': STA4 1547–48 (CWA, p. 225), banner bearers, bell ringers, with 'our offeryng at our lady churche'; STA9 1557–58 (CWA, p. 279), banner and cope bearers, bell ringers,

drink and offering; STA 10 1559–60 (CWA, p. 280), banner bearers, bell ringers and offering. The absence of any record of procession before 1547 (cf. St. Edmund's smoke farthings' procession 1518–44) may be related to St. Thomas's appropriation to the cathedral chapter, until c. 1539. Until that time the parish was possibly exempt from customary pentecostal payments, or, if paid, the sums may not have been itemized in the procurator's accounts. Royal injunctions of 1547 included prohibition of processions, chiefly aimed at Sunday and feast day processions at mass. Thereafter, St. Thomas's Whitsun procession occurs only in 1557 and 1559 after Mary's reign saw the reaffirmation of processions -- 'the formal expression of the identity of the parish' (Eamon Duffy, *The Stripping of the Altars: Traditional Religion in England c. 1400–1580*, New Haven and London, Yale University Press, 1992, p 532).

19 *Trepidantes* is related to *tripudium* or its variants, glossed in early medieval British sources as 'jubilation', but from the fifteenth century (e.g. *triputo, tripido*) as 'to dance' (*Revised Medieval Latin Word-List from British and Irish Sources*, prepared by R. E. Latham, London, Oxford University Press, 1965, p. 495). Payments for Frick Friday: STF1-7 1478–98, STF10 1503, STF13-16 1507–14, STF22-23 1523–38, *uxores* -- alternatively *matrones, mulieres*; STF1 1478, STF3-12 1488–1505, STF16-21 1514–21, *servientes* -- alternatively *domicellae, ancillae, puellae servientes*; STF1-23 1478–1538, *filiae*; STF1-15 1478–1513, STF17-21 1517–21, *scholares* -- alternatively *pueri*.

20 Backman, *Religious Dances*, p. 95.

21 In 1517, for example, the celebration was presided over by Master Thomas Martin, noted under 'Allocationes pro Administracione' as officiating at all the accustomed feasts in the parish throughout the year (STF17 1516–17). For comparison with the dancers' rewards: banner bearers in Whit Thursday processions at St. Edmund's received, as a group, 7d in 1482–83 and 3d in 1538–39; a carpenter mending a gutter received 6d per day in each of these years (under 'Custus', CWA, p. 29; 'Payments', p. 84).

22 St Thomas's fabric accounts record payments for 'scholars' until Whitsun 1521 -- from 1523 'pueri' (STA21-2). The term 'scholars' may primarily refer to students at De Vaux college in Salisbury or pupils at the local grammar school, though this would not preclude their also comprising (or including) local sons. The college, founded in 1262 for twenty scholars, numbered nine 'fellows' in 1542 -- in 1526 all but two students had been ordered to take up residence in Oxford or other universities. The undergraduate body was probably youthful -- one scholar's admission in 1473 was conditional on completing his education in grammar, perhaps at the

local grammar school, whose last headmaster was appointed in 1470. There does not seem to have been a separate school for choristers during this period (VCH, *Wiltshire*, vol. VI, p. 77; vol. III, p. 180).

23 Cf. Rosalind Miles, *The Women's History of the World*, London, Paladin, 1989: 'It is hard to find any culture where women as a group did not enjoy some form of the space or freedom that was denied to them as individuals' (p. 126).

24 Often extending to two days (the second Monday and Tuesday after Easter Sunday), Hocktide involved mock ransom sums payable between men and women; it was adopted as a means of fund raising in various English parishes. St. Edmund's first recorded receipt of Hock money, given towards a new window, occurs in 1497 (CWA, p. 47). In 1510, St. Edmund's women collected 4s 'ad commodum ecclesie', but 3s 4d was spent on a meal for them (CWA, p. 56, and Allocations, p. 57). Both Hock and Whitsun events may thus have had a transitional stage where participants controlled the destination of the money gathered, assigning it, for example, variously for community or church purposes on an ad hoc basis.

25 STA12 1545–46 (labelled in error 1595–96); STA3 1546–47; STA9 1557–58; STA10 1559–60: receipts for Hocktide and Friday in Whit week, 'by hands of our wives and us and for gathering of sons, daughters and servants' or similar; STA10 1561–62, and annual accounts 1567–68 to 1570–71: 'men's and women's gathering at Hocktide'.

26 STA10, annual accounts 1571–72 (Hock only), 1572–73 to 1580–81 (Hock and Whitsun). Hocktide celebrations disappear in all three parishes after 1581, suggestive of a ban imposed by higher church authorities.

27 STA10, individual accounts 1577–78 to 1579–80: 'Ralph [Ridgeley] for guiding the children on dancing day' or similar.

28 Whitsun receipts: STA10, individual accounts 1592–93 to 1597–98 and 1599–1600, gathered in Whit week over and above charges for children's dance; STA13 1598–99, receipts book p. 10, minstrels, bell ringers; STA16 1601–02, children; STA16, 13 accounts 1602–03 to 1619–20, Whit gatherings; STA16 1620–21, last sum for Whitsun money. Late sixteenth-century Puritan sermons condemned dance where as a male/female occasion it was conducive to adultery (Davies, *Liturgical Dance*, pp. 30-32); perhaps in response to this, St. Thomas's confined its dance to children in the last decade of the century.

29 WRO, St. Martin's: 1899/65, Churchwardens' Accounts bound in one volume 1567–1653, with gaps [SMA1; my foliation]; 1899/66, copy (1904) of Churchwardens' Accounts 1642–1700, with some earlier material [SMA2]. Under Receipts: Hock, SMA1 fol. 1r 1567–68, fol. 5r 1568–69, fol. 11r 1580–81, fol. 15r 1581–82 (sum blank); Whitsun

dance/dancing money, SMA1 fol. 7r 1568–69, fol. 11r 1580–81, fol. 51v 1593–94; Whitsun dance/dancing, SMA1 fol. 15r 1581–82, fol. 25r 1588–89, fol. 40v 1590–91; SMA2 p. 243 1597–98; SMA1 fol. 92r 1606–07; Whitsun dancers, SMA1 fol. 31r 1589–90, fol. 44r ?1592–93; last Whitsun gathering, SMA1 fol. 138r 1624–25.

30 'No Whitsun Dance shall be suffered hereafter to come into ye Cath.' Chur. nor into ye cloyster, or elsewhere near ye said Ch: in time of Divine Service' (Salisbury Chapter Muniments, Press 2, Sessions Book for the Close 1613–34/35 transcribed in Isaac Walton's Collections, vol. V, p. 268). My thanks to Suzanne Eward, archivist and librarian, Salisbury Cathedral, for this citation.

31 WRO 2007/35, a sworn record of ancient customs pertaining to Great Wishford and Barford, 1603, fol. [3v], numbers 17-18; VCH, *Wiltshire*, vol. VI, pp. 140-41, Whitsun fairs.

32 CWA, p. xv; SEA4 1538–39 (CWA, p. 83), 13s received of the gathering of the 'wyffes dawnse' (under subheading of the same name); SEA5 *temp.* Henry VIII (CWA, p. 87, suggesting 1541–42), 4s paid to the waits for the wives' dance; SEA5 *temp.* Henry VIII (CWA, pp. 80-81), 3s 6d to the minstrels for 'the wiefes' [i.e. wives' dance, or light]; SEA7 1556–57 (CWA, p. 101), payment to minstrels for bringing the wives' light to church. Waits were also paid for 'bryngyng in' the wives' light at St. Thomas's (STA3 1546–47 [CWA, p. 274]).

33 The complex issues of this period have been fully documented by Paul Slack, "Poverty and Politics in Salisbury: 1597–1666", in Peter Clark and Paul Slack [eds.], *Crisis and Order in English Towns 1500–1700*, Toronto, University of Toronto Press, 1972, whose conclusions shape the context of the discussion that follows. See also Paul Slack, "Police and People", in *The Impact of Plague in Tudor and Stuart England*, Oxford, Oxford University Press, 1990 [revised edition], pp. 284-310, for discussion of the social strains that plague brought to urban populations -- from the breakdown of neighbourly ties induced by fear of infection to protest and disorder consequent upon municipal efforts to isolate and control the sick.

34 Borthwick and Chandler, *Our Chequered Past*, p. 63: St. Martin's parish lay in the southeast of the city, an area which 'remained an undeveloped backwater until the nineteenth century'; its boundaries took in the cattle market, leather working (notably tanners) and prostitution (centred in Culver Street -- cf. WRO G23/1/1, Salisbury Corporation Ledger A, fol. 158r); SMA2, p. 248, memorandum on Whitsun income (with reference to Launcelet Davies, churchwarden ?1598–99).

35 The sum of 10s was gathered in each year (CWA, pp. 158-59 and 161).

36 Slack, "Poverty and Politics", p. 180, note 49. St. Thomas's (STA 16), for example, gathered nothing in the period 1604–05 'by reason of the sicknes'; no sums are entered under the Whitsun account heading for 1605–06, 1606–07 and 1610–11. On the other hand, St. Martin's continued to gather substantial sums at Whitsun (between 40s and 60s per annum) in the first quarter of the seventeenth century -- twelve entries, SMA 1, fol. 73r 1602–03 to fol. 169r 1624–25.

37 Cf. the midsummer procession of the Salisbury Tailors Guild which, by 1611, had moved from a fifteenth-century para-liturgical context (celebration of the midsummer obit) to become an unruly event, offensive to the incumbent Sabbatarian mayor (see Audrey Douglas, "Midsummer in Salisbury: the Tailors' Guild and Confraternity 1444–1642", *Renaissance and Reformation* 25 (1989) pp. 35-51).

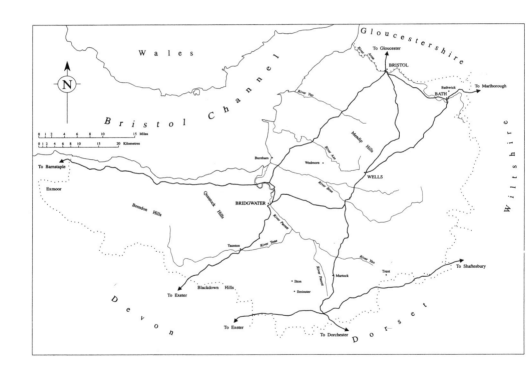

Figure 5

Locations in Somerset where professional bear/bull baiters lived

Bull and Bear Baiting in Somerset: The Gentles' Sport

James Stokes

Current research into English dramatic records includes baitings as a category of entertainments, and duly extracts the many references to bull and bear baiting that continue to turn up there (see the indexes to the *Records of Early English Drama* volumes for the many references). Yet perhaps because baitings are so alien to a modern sensibility, there has been little systematic attempt to explore their nature, implications, and significance, especially as they occurred in the provinces. In the county of Somerset baitings are among the most frequently occurring items, turning up in nearly every class of record (see Figure 5). This paper is an attempt to come to terms with that evidence in relation to entertainment traditions as a whole in Somerset.

The Baiters Themselves

A variety of evidence suggests that numerous professional bear and bull baiters operated within the county. The civic records of Bridgwater contain several payments to bearwards between 1537–38 and 1581–82. Some were traveling professionals, such as the Marquess of Dorset's bearward in 1537–38, the Earl of Bath's bearward in 1542–43, an unnamed Lord in 1572–73, and the Lord Compton's and the Queen's bearwards in 1581–82.[1] Several others are unidentified. One, a Harry the Bearward (identity otherwise unknown) was paid twice, 1540–41 and 1543–44.[2] Several professional bearwards are also recorded in Bath, including Warwick's bearward in 1575–76; the Queen's bearward in 1592–93 and her bearwards in 1601–02 (curiously, the single bearward was paid twice as much as those in 1601–02); and Dudley's bearward in 1593–94. Another professional who sounds as if he were local was John Chapman, paid in 1576–77.[3] The travel patterns of these professionals are obscure. Dorset's Bearward and his players were both paid in the same year at Bridgwater; and in one three-year sequence, an unidentified bearward or bearwards each received exactly the same amount of 3s 4d in payment. But none of the bearwards were paid during the same year at Bridgwater and at Bath, so no conclusion about their patterns of travel can be drawn. In 1605, a suit in the bishop's court charged that 'the bearwards' stayed at a woman's house in Wells, and that she then followed them to Bristol, suggesting a route that was in part north-south and further suggesting that on this occasion several bearwards were traveling together.[4]

Several others were identifiably local bearwards (see Figure 6). Robert Midlam of Burnham (eight miles from Bridgwater) was presented for holding a bear baiting in late summer 1574 at the backside of his house, thereby drawing many parishioners away from a sermon by the vicar. From the church they could hear 'the noys of the Beares and dogges fyghting'. According to one witness, Midlam 'manie & sundry times kept beare baytinge in the parishe'; other witnesses referred to the 'bears', indicating that Midlam kept more than one. Midlam had confronted the vicar, accusing him of trying to hinder his 'game' by scheduling the sermon at the same time as the baiting.[5]

Hugh Palmer, of Martock, was cited in the bishop's court 'ffor leadinge of his beare abroad aboute the cuntrie & beatinge of the same vppon the sabboathe daie./.', apparently at East Pennard in September 1620 (about ten to twelve miles from home).[6] Richard Lucock, a butcher (formerly of Kingsbury, Somerset, of Ilminster when arrested, but described as a vagabond), was cited at the Quarter Sessions in 1606 for traveling from place to place in the county and baiting his bears with dogs.[7] Three others who habitually kept bear and bull baitings, and may or may not themselves have been bearwards, were Richard Mayne and Robert Moris, of Wedmore, cited in 1582 for keeping bear baitings on the sabboth; and Abraham Brokes of Trent (a parish now in Dorset), cited in 1622 for bear and bull baitings that drew great disordered companies.[8]

Several local professional bull baiters also appear in the records. Thomas Nehellyng of Ilton, twenty-four years of age, kept three fighting bulls and, between 1607 and 1608 traveled with them to watches and ales in Somerset, Dorset, and Wiltshire. Sometimes he stayed two days and held several baitings for which he charged a set fee; he seems to have had a partner, John Alway in his travels. At the quarter sessions he was whipped for being a vagrant and ordered to desist.[9] William Powell, the rector of Bathwick, admitted in 1610 to keeping a baiting bull of his own and baiting it in Bathwick and at Bath.[10] Four of these seven local baiters lived in the southwest part of the county, and all the locations but one were near a major roadway, through Wedmore (the exception) was nearly equidistant between a number of major Somerset towns in central Somerset. Given the great number of baitings recorded in the county, and their wide geographical distribution, it seems probable that there were other local baiters as well.

Baiting and Ales

Most of the recorded baitings in Somerset occur in court records as part of attempts to suppress church ales. The context of the court records creates three principal impressions about baitings. The first is that the justices of the peace viewed these baitings as an integral component of church ales; it would seem that for many wardens they were the entertainment of choice. In Isle Abbotts, for example, when the churchwarden's accounts were passed one year, the new warden was later presented for having said:

> Wee will haue noe more rates heere, but wee will have beare beateing, and haue the beare to stake, and make him roare, hee him selfe then roreing as if itt had byn a beare att stake …[11]

In Publow, a new churchwarden similarly earned himself a day in court by proclaiming to his fellow warden in the chancel of the church:

> Thou art a Baker, & I am a brewer, [kh] thou keepe a bare, & I will keepe a bull, & wee will [ba] keepe a church ale, and because people shall haue sporte enough for theire monie wee will haue a a sh[...] meaninge a whoare.[12]

In West Bradley a churchwarden was presented for causing a female bear to be brought into the churchyard with dogs at its heels, and lodged in the church house, where it terrified an old woman who was trapped inside with it.[13]

The second impression is that the wardens did not make the bulk of their money from the baitings themselves; I have found no evidence of admission being charged, though it may well have been. Rather, wardens used the baitings to attract drinkers who spent lots of money on ale brewed by the wardens for the event. A number of suppression orders specifically complained that the cost of corn was high because of the vast amounts being used in brewing for the ales. In Ilton, for example, one Richard Wembridge was presented for keeping 'ale to sell & Bull Baytinge to thuse of the said parishe', as was William Bicknell of Isle Brewers.[14]

And third, the baitings, as used by wardens, could have a communal dimension, in celebration of old playing traditions and the old religion, that troubled reform-minded authorities. In Merriott, the churchwarden was presented for keeping a church ale with bull *and* bear baitings, during which (in an interesting bit of symbolism) he brought

> the said communyon cuppe out to the beare stake while the [beatynge] beare was at the stake, and there made the companye to drynke his Ale howse beare in the communyon cuppe, and [there] made the communyon cup to be a common drynkeing cup at his beare baytinge./ ...[15]

This social dimension of baiting can also be seen in a complaint by the judges of Assize at Bath in 1638 that even at that late date there were

> gathering great Companies of vnrulie people at Bull baiting*es* vnder the pre*t*ense of helping some poore man ... soe publique and soe frequent in most places of this County that it cannot bee vnknowen to the Iustices of Peace ...[16]

Tipplers, alehouse keepers, and other local entrepreneurs within the county used baitings in the same ways -- as a form of entertainment to attract spenders. John Hooper, a tippler from Huntspill, had for many years held bull and bear baitings twice a year -- one on May Day and one on 'parting*es* Mundaye' -- when servants and other young people were at liberty to attend. These were 'cryed' (that is, advertised) games 'pr*o*claimed in three seuerall [Markett] Townes at the least'. He also kept minstrels to lure the young people to spend money on drink.[17] Abraham Brokes alias Thorne, a tippler from Trent was presented before the justices because he

> hath brewed and sold ale in great abundance, and by reason of his bull -- and beare -- baytings hath lately drawne much disordred company thither./ ...[18]

The law required that bulls be baited before slaughter (to tenderize the meat) and in 1611–12 four butchers were presented by the city of Wells sessions court for failing to do so. Three more were similarly presented in 1613–14.[19] So initially it apparently was not the baitings in themselves that were the main target of the justices, but their being held in connection with ales, revels, and other entertainments.

This linkage between baitings and traditional entertainments can be seen in several other ways as well. Most of the recorded baitings occurred, logically enough, between May and October, when people could comfortably congregate out of doors, and when most ales, wakes, and revels were held. The greatest number of presentments for baiting (twelve each) occurred in May and June; the next greatest number (eight each) in July, August, and September. Two each were reported in March and October, and none in February, April, or November. Two seasonal exceptions are recorded. A bull baiting occurred in Bedminster on St. John Evangelist's Day (27 December 1634); and in December 1579 the mayor of Bridgwater paid 3s 4d to a bearward.[20] Most of the presentments in May and June mention the baitings in connection with Whitsun or Midsummer ales, those in July through August with ales, revels, and the feasts of local patron saints.

Many baitings and ales must traditionally have been held on Sundays because all but one presentment during the sixteenth century accused the baiter of violating the sabbath. The earliest surviving presentment for baiting, from 1555, is typical: a man from Chewton was presented in the bishop's court for habitually keeping bull baitings during the time of divine service.[21] During the 1580s and 1590s the number of similar presentments increased significantly. The quarter sessions issued its first surviving orders suppressing church ales in 1594 and 1596.[22] In Bridgwater -- an increasingly puritan town -- bearwards permanently disappeared from civic records following payments by the mayor to the queen's bearward in 1581–82, a time coinciding with the surge of sabbatarian attacks on traditional entertainments in England.

During the first decade of the seventeenth century many parishes moved their ales and baitings from Sundays to another day of the week. Of twenty-seven presentments for baiting between 1601 and 1610, all but two of the baitings had occurred as part of church ales, tipplings, or other ales, and not one was held on a Sunday. Seventeen of those twenty-seven presentments occurred in 1602 as part of a major crackdown by the justices on ales and baitings -- whatever their form. All seventeen of these baitings (see Figure 7) had occurred in communities near Bridgwater and Taunton, an area with resident justices who strongly opposed traditional parish fund-raising entertainments, and most of the seventeen baitings were connected with Ascension, Whitsun, or Midsummer Ales. In 1603, thirteen more presentments in the same area were made in the six months following the death of Queen Elizabeth I, although whether the timing of the crackdown was connected with her death is by no means clear. The two bear baitings among these seventeen presentments were in parishes seven to ten miles apart (Enmore and North Curry).[23]

During the rest of the decade (1605–10), as the map shows, the radius of presentments gradually expanded to other parts of the county, and appears to have targeted professional bearwards and bull keepers who lived there. In 1608, the justices of the peace -- including the bishop and cathedral officials -- issued an expanded quarter sessions order that for the first time specifically prohibited bull and bear baiting.[24] It also specified for the first time that those who *attended* such events would be punished as well. In the same year (1608), the assize judges ordered constables of the hundreds to inquire of churchwardens whether brewings were being held in their jurisdictions for baitings and ales.[25] But the suppressions were selective. Two parishes near Bridgwater (Chilton and Spaxton) were presented late in the decade for baitings and ales, but professional bearwards en route to Bristol apparently stopped at Wells in 1605 without encountering any trouble from the authorities in that cathedral city.[26]

In the next decade (1611–20), as the map shows, all the presentments were against parishes in parts of the county not included in earlier waves of presentments. Most were for baitings held at ales and revels on the sabbath or on local revel days; all occurred during the summer; nearly half involved bears. Clearly professional bearwards were continuing to travel between 1611 and 1620 in parts of the county remote from the Bridgwater area. One of them who lived at Martock travelled twelve miles to a baiting on the sabbath at East Pennard.[27]

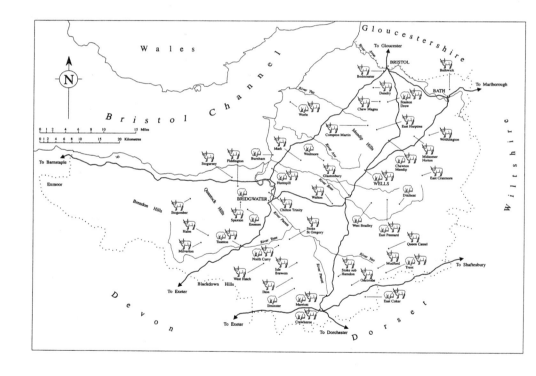

Figure 6

Evidence of Somerset Bull and Bear Baiting

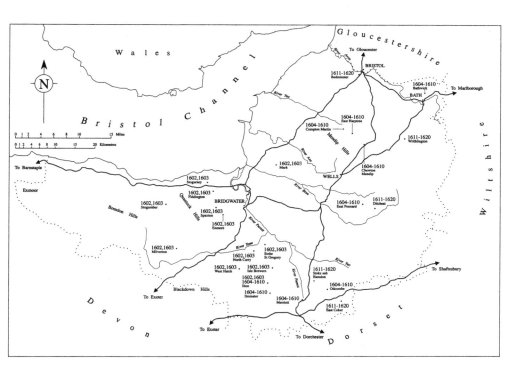

Figure 7
Pattern of Presentments for Bull or Bear Baitings, 1602–20

During the next decade (1621–30), bulls, bears, and church ales returned to the very areas around Bridgwater and Taunton that had been so heavily suppressed in 1602 and 1603. In 1621 at West Hatch the churchwardens were presented for a Whitsun ale and baiting just as they had been twenty years earlier.[28] A tippler in Huntspill near Burnham was presented for multi-parish ales and baitings on feasts and holidays, extending the evidence for bear baitings in that area to a fifty-year period during which they were, to some degree, resistant to suppression orders.[29] In 1623 a churchwarden in Isle Abbotts near Taunton vowed to procure a bear for church ales.[30] In 1628, at the request of six ministers, the judges of the Assize reissued their earlier order suppressing ales and baitings, and requiring that the order be published annually on the first Sunday in February.[31]

In the next decade (1631–40), the Assize judges again renewed the order of 1632 suppressing baitings and ales, but the king forced them to rescind their order in 1633.[32] An Assize order at Bath in 1638 complained that bull baitings to help poor men, and attracting great companies of people, were 'so public and so frequent' that the justices of the peace could not fail to be aware of them.[33] Several wardens were cited for an equal number of bear and bull baitings during this decade, all of which suggests that the suppressions were a failure, though improper observance of the sabbath or misuse of church properties was still an issue.

The Nature of the Baitings
In Somerset there is nothing so elegant as the payment in the Devon records to a servant of the Duke of Suffolk with 'the dancing bear and the dancing wife'.[34] Instead, the fragmentary descriptions that survive suggest a basic and brutal activity in which a bear or bull was chained then baited with dogs, or led about tormented by dogs. Several references survive to bull rings in Bridgwater and Taunton, as well as in other towns. The one in Bridgwater seems to have been an enclosed wooden structure and others

seemed to have been like earthen amphitheatres.[35] In other places, perhaps in most other places, the bear was simply tied to a stake. There survives in Axbridge a four-foot metal stake with five barbed heads that was anchored in the ground to keep the bull from escaping.[36] In Burnham in 1574, parishioners in the church could 'heare the noys of the Beares and dogges fyghting togeathers at midlams doore'. At Ilminster, a butcher and itinerant bearward was accused of baiting his bears with dogs ('*cum canibus* vapulabat Angli*ce with* Dogg*es* did beate'). In Writhlington in 1619, a man admitted to attending 'a litle sporte of a bull with dogges in the evening after evening prayer./' In Midsummer Norton in 1622 the bull baiting occurred in the morning; and in Merriott in 1620, the bear was described as being 'at the stake'. The professional baiter presented at Ilton had traveled to ales and watches with 'fyghting bulls'. In Isle Abbotts, the newly chosen warden boasted to the parishioners that the bear he would get would be made to 'roare'.[37]

Several records suggest that bulls were sometimes baited at the same events with bears, and that the events themselves, such as an ale with baitings, could continue over two or more days. That was the case at East Coker in 1617, and at Huntspill on May Day in 1623.[38] The most bizarre baiting occurred at Taunton in 1590 when a group of armed revellers went to the house of a local bearward at midnight and demanded that he bring his bear to the ring in the market square to be beaten. When he refused, they seized the bear and led it through the streets of Taunton and neighbouring villages, letting it run loose so that residents were terrified, as the complainant says, 'out of theire wittes and fallen madd'. Then for some three hours the revellers 'with dogges and other devises and whippes and whelebarrowes, beate the said beare, but did not tye the said beare' rather beating him loose. At one point, it was claimed, they took the bear into a house and frightened a woman who was great with child.[39] All the evidence suggests that baiting in Somerset was a cruel and violent form of taunting and combat with the potential for real danger to all concerned. It was also extremely popular and survived in Somerset, as elsewhere, into the nineteenth century, when it was outlawed by Parliament.[40]

The Symbolic Dimension of Baiting

Recent scholarship has convincingly shown that baiting was a rich source of metaphor in the custom, theatre, and religion of this period.[41] It seems to have been in Somerset too, as the activities of the churchwardens cited above make clear. A Star Chamber case of 1604 charged that three men were presented, apparently in 1603, 'for playeing Christmas sportes in a beares skinne at the house of one Edward Keynes esquier', in either North Cadbury, South Cadbury, or Sparkford (the case is unclear on that point). An opponent of this Christmas sport charged in his bill of complaint that the local justice of the peace who had jurisdiction hid away the charges and failed to bring them to the quarter sessions.[42] The nature and meaning of this particular Christmas game is not clear, but E. C. Cawte describes a number of mimetic Christmas customs on the continent in which revelers dressed as bears and acted out what seem to have been mock combat and baiting plays, similar in nature and purpose to mummers' plays used for parish collections and perhaps similar to this one.[43]

The metaphorical use of baiting in attacks upon women is particularly curious. It was used to intimidate, as by the man who seized his wife and 'threatened to tye her to the Bullring on the Cornehill at Taunton and there woulde beat her with dogges'.[44] Two men at Leigh Upon Mendip were accused with others of breaking up a house where they 'violentlie tooke a woman, or mayde thereof, and termed her to bee theire beare'. They were said to have carried a piece of her smock through town as if it were a flag. Saying that 'theire beare was over heete, and must be cooled', they all threw a cup of beer 'in her bare tayle'.[45] This particularly scurrilous example seems a curiously ritualized attack on the woman, but also suggests their image of what must have happened to bears at the stake -- baiting them to the point of a dangerous frenzy, and shows imagery of baiting to have been part of their vernacular. Other incidents in which bears had terrified women were mentioned earlier in the paper (the pregnant woman in Taunton; the old lady frighted in the church house).

Imagery associating bears, especially headless ones, with the devil was common in the rhetoric of puritans, who condemned baiting as a heathen activity, saying 'the Deuill is the Maister of the game, beareward and all'.[46] The most vivid example of baiting so used metaphorically in Somerset occurs in a sermon, published in 1584, concerning a woman's encounter with a headless bear in Ditcheat, Somerset. The woman had come home from a trip to Gloucester foaming at the mouth and claiming that a headless bear had followed her into the yard. After she had been abed for several days, a great noise arose as if several carts were approaching, and, according to the sermon, a bear with no head or tail came into the room by her bed. It struck the woman three times on the feet and took her from the bed, then 'thrust the womans hed betwixt her legges, and so roulled her in a rounde compasse like a Hoope through three other Chambers', and down the stairs. The creature then disappeared, but when a window was opened, 'the womans legges [were] after a marveilous maner thrust out at the windowe, so that they were clasped about the post in the middle of the window dowe ...' Her husband and son demanded, in the name of the Father, Son and Holy Ghost, that the thing leave, which it did as an apparition of a child appeared. The woman claimed it to have been the devil, caused to appear by her sins, and she was thereafter protected by many learned men.[47] The bizarre aspects of this description aside, it illustrates the powerful presence of the bear as a religious metaphor in sixteenth-century Somerset.

The copious evidence in Somerset -- a county that one assumes to have been typical -- shows that baitings were central to the entertainments and the culture of the county, for all classes, and for all sizes of community. One cannot fairly and accurately describe traditional entertainments there without acknowledging and understanding the part that baitings played, and the hold that baiting had on the imagination of the people. The creature to be baited seems to have symbolized any force, excess, loss of control, or danger that must be engaged and subdued. It was the opposite of reason and order. And, strange though it may seem, baiting was a form of comic allegory revealing qualities of character, and exhibiting elements of plot in its reversals, surprises, and rough justice.

Notes

1   Somerset Record Office [hereafter SRO]: D/B/bw 1451, fol. 12v; 1436, fol. 7; 1469, fol. 6v; 1474, fols. 10, 2v.

2   For Harry the Bearward, see SRO: D/B/bw 1441, fol. 20, and 1442, fol. 17v. For other unidentified bearwards, see SRO: D/B/bw 1461, fol. 10 (paid in 1561–62); 1564, fol. 4 (paid in 1579–80); and 1566, fol. 3v (paid in 1580–81).

3   For these references I would like to thank Robert Alexander, whose dramatic records of Bath will appear in the forthcoming *Records of Early English Drama* volume for Somerset. See BRO: CA No. 5, mb [1]; No. 31, mb [1]; No. 41, mb [1]; No. 32, mb [1]; SJ No. 6, mb [1].

4   SRO: D/D/Cd 36, pp. 382-83, 385, 476-78.

5   SRO: D/D/Cd 15, fols. 169v, 136v, 132v-133.

6   SRO: D/D/Ca 231, fol. 193v.

7   SRO: QSI 11, part 1, fol. 103.

8   Wells Cathedral Library: shelf X2, Dean's Consistory Court Book, fol. [7]; SRO: QSR 41, part 1, fol. 48.

9   SRO: QSR 37, part 2, fol. 101A.

10   SRO: D/D/Ca 155, fol. [58]; D/D/Ca 163, fols. 217v-218.

11   SRO: D/D/Cd 58, fol. [26v].

12   SRO: D/D/Ca 330, fol. 17.

13   SRO: D/D/Ca 330, fol. 163.

14   SRO: QSI 7, fol. 55.

15   SRO: DD/TMP 8, fol. [21v].

16   PRO: SP 16/395, single sheet.

17   SRO: QSR 43, part 1, fols. 78r-v.

18   SRO: QSR 41, part 1, fol. 48.

19   Wells Town Hall: Sessions Book 1, fols. [147v], [17r-v].

20   SRO: D/D/Ca 294, fol. 339; D/B/bw 1564. For transcriptions of the many baitings summarized here and below and full citations, see the indexes to the forthcoming *REED* volume for Somerset.

21 SRO: D/D/Ca 25, p. 66.

22 William Prynne, Canterburies Doome. Wing: p. 3917, p. 152.

23 SRO: QSI 7, fol. 11, 54.

24 SRO: QSR 2, fol. 118.

25 SRO: DD/HI 459, packet 1, item six, single sheet.

26 SRO: QSI 16, fol. 64; QSI 7, fol. 50; QSI 10, part 1, fol. 49; SRO: D/D/Cd 36, pp. 382-83, 385, 476-78.

27 SRO: QSI 8, fol. 94.

28 SRO: QSR 38, fol. 94.

29 SRO: QSR 43, part 1, fol. 78.

30 SRO: D/D/Cd 58, fol. [26v].

31 SRO: QSR 61, part 1, fol. 47.

32 PRO: ASSI 24/20, part 1, fols. 49v-50; PRO: SP 16/25, single sheet.

33 PRO: SP 16/395.

34 See John Wasson [ed.], *Records of Early English Drama: Devon*, Toronto, University of Toronto Press, 1986, p. 223.

35 SRO: D/B/bw 1606, fol. 7; SRO: QSR 8, fol. 80. Evidence of bull rings or pits, some similar to amphitheatres, is cited in Robin Atthill, *Old Mendip*, London, 1964, for Buckland Dinham (p. 178), Charterhouse-on-Mendip (p. 179), Stoke St. Michael (p. 180), and Hinton Charterhouse (p. 181); in Ethelbert Horne, "Bull-Rings and Cock-Pits", for Buckland Newton (p. 218) and E. M. Troyte Bullock, "Bull Rings", 'for East Coker (p. 291) in *Notes and Queries for Somerset and Dorset* 17 (1923). On bull and bear rings as proto-theatres, see Glynne Wickham, *Early English Stages*, New York, 1969, vol 2, part 1, pp. 161-71; and J. Leeds Barroll, *The Revels History of Drama in English*, London, 1975, vol 3, pp. 124-28.

36 H. St. George Gray, *Somersetshire Archaeological and Natural Society Proceedings* 91 (1946), p. 27.

37 SRO: D/D/Cd 15, fol. 169v; QSI 11, part 1, fol. 103; D/D/Ca 209, fol. 201v; D/D/Cd 58, fol. [23v]; DD/TMP 8, fol. [21v]; QSR 37, part 2, fol. 101A; D/D/Cd 58, fol. [26v].

38 SRO: QSR 29, fols. 10r-v; QSR 43, part 1, fol. 78.

39 PRO: STAC 5/S 61/12, single membrane.

40 For descriptions of baitings in Somerset (their route and manner) as they survived into the nineteenth century, see Gray, pp. 27-28 (Axbridge); J. H. Porter, "Beastly Baiting", *Devon and Cornwall Notes and Queries* 36 (1987), pp. 54-58 (Pensford); E. M. Church, *Ye Olde Wells Fair*, n.p. [Wells], n.d., pp. 8-12 (Wells, the most detailed description of a civic-sponsored baiting).

41 See Stephen Dickey, "Shakespeare's Mastiff Comedy", *Shakespeare*

Quarterly 42 (1991), pp. 255-75; and Alexander Leggatt, "Shakespeare
and Bearbaiting", Tetsuo Kishi, Roger Pringle, and Stanley Well [eds.],
Shakespeare and Cultural Traditions, Newark, 1991, pp. 43-53. For
older but valuable studies, see indexes to E. K. Chambers, *The Elizabethan Stage*, London, 1923, 4 vols; and G. E. Bentley, *The Jacobean
and Caroline Stage*, London, 1941, 8 vols. For plays using bears, see
Arvin H. Jupin [ed.], *Mucedorus*, London, 1987; "Oberon: The Fairy
Prince", in Stephen Orgel, *Ben Jonson: Selected Masques*, New Haven,
1970, pp. 101-15.

42 PRO: STAC 8/43/3, single sheet.
43 E. C. Cawte, *Ritual Animal Disguise*, Cambridge, 1978, pp. 199-207. On
the ancient origins of animal games, including those involving represen-
tation of bears, and their uses in traditional English entertainments, see
E. K. Chambers, *The Medieval Stage*, Oxford 1903, vol. 1, pp. 64-73,
116-21, 136-43, 160-69, 255-63; Christina Hole, *English Sports and
Pastimes*, London, 1949, pp. 97-110; and Joseph Strutt, *The Sports
and Pastimes of the People of England*, London, 1903, pp. xlvii-xlix,
186-87, 195-215, 306.
44 SRO: QSR 8, fol. 80.
45 SRO: D/D/Ca 240, fol. 119.
46 Phillip Stubbes, *The Anatomy of Abuses*, London, 1583, sign. P2v.
S.T.C. No. 23376.
47 Margaret Cooper, *A True and Most Dreadfull Discourse of a Woman
Possessed with the Deuill*, London, 1584; rpt Weston-super-Mare, 1886.
BL C27a 6 (Pollard and Redgrave No. 5681, p. 126).

'Anye disguised persons':
Parish Entertainment in West Yorkshire

Barbara D. Palmer

Because the old West Riding at some 1,776,064 statute acres, seven deaneries, two peculiars, and nearly two hundred parishes covers such a broad geographic and cultural territory, one would expect the surviving parish entertainment records to reflect that breadth, which they do. Already noted in print or previous conference papers has been the abundance of professional, civic and great household entertainment in the West Riding, as well as the extensive entertainment communication between southern and northern England. What has not been sufficiently noted is West Riding parish entertainment activity, for which the records are relatively plentiful and refreshingly detailed. The records run from the fourteenth through the seventeenth centuries, documenting some three hundred years of northern folk assemblies.

Common to those assemblies are the church injunctions and cause papers prohibiting them, most notably the 1548 Deanery of Doncaster injunction and the 1571 and 1612 West Riding injunctions, to say nothing of the various York archbishopric visitation and cause paper distresses which punctuate the period under consideration. None of these prohibitions seems to have made the least bit of difference to the parish inhabitants. Regardless of such phrases as 'shall not suffer', 'suppressing of', 'hinder and prevent', and so forth, the folk of the West Riding parishes continued to meet and greet each other in a variety of convivial assemblies. Moreover, the church's injunctions, prohibitions, excommunications and punishments seem to have been ignored on a regular basis by almost everyone everywhere in the West Riding, regard-

less of social class, economic class, gender, age and religious lean-
ing.

The largest category of surviving West Riding parish records
documents activities during the four summer months of May
through August: May games, summer games and rushbearings.
The earliest extant account is Wistow's 'summer game', held by
the young people of the town on 18 June 1469, Trinity Sunday.[1]
Quite clearly from the depositions, there was no trouble about the
summer game itself: the case is a suit between two people rather
than an office proceeding. Margaret More, a maiden of Wistow,
seems to be suing someone for defaming her character, charging
that she behaved suspiciously with someone else in one William
Barker's house on 18 June. Her defense, and the reason for history's serendipitous good fortune, is that she could not have been in
William Barker's house on 18 June because

> on the immediately previous Sunday that very Margaret had been
> chosen by the above-mentioned young people as queen in the above-
> mentioned game for the Sunday mentioned in the article. This game
> ... was held on that very Sunday in a barn of one John Dudman of
> Wistow, located near and next to the churchyard of the same church,
> at which [barn] ... the said Margaret, coming before the twelfth hour,
> that is the noon hour, of the same day, stayed continuously from that
> same hour until after sunset the same day, holding and occupying the
> queen's throne.[2]

From the depositions, which concur in all detail, one learns a lot
about a West Riding summer game. First, it repeatedly is described as 'the custom of the countryside there', a typical 'summer
pastime'. The king and queen are chosen 'by lot', whatever that
means, and they must be unmarried: 'on the immediately following Sunday the said Thomas Barker married one Agnes at Sherburn-in-Elmet as is the custom and therefore afterwards the
above-mentioned Thomas Barker did not any longer exercise the
office of king in the aforesaid game', a statement which seems to
imply that the king's and queen's roles could continue after the

actual game. Between eleven and noon on the day, a group of young people went to Margaret's and Thomas' respective houses to escort them, preceded by music, to John Dudman's barn, called 'summer house' and 'where that game had usually been held for some years past ...'. In addition to Margaret's holding court on her throne from noon 'until after sunset, ... attending to that very game and making herself agreeable in the same in a decent way then as seemed suitable to the same [game]', we also learn of one young man who plays 'both steward and butler in the above-mentioned game', two young men who play knights and 'attended at all times upon the queen', and over a hundred other participants, 'both men and young women ...'.

Although the Wistow account is more detailed than any other of which I am aware, it is representative in at least one respect: as long as summer games, May games and rushbearings were not disruptive, they seem to have been sanctioned. This point, I think, is important. Because the surviving accounts largely record some sort of mayhem, care must be taken not to necessarily assign blame to 'folk entertainments' more rightfully assigned to 'the folk' themselves. Several instances serve. In 1589, the three 'gardiani de Borobrigge ... are inioyned to chuse there lord of somer in some other place then church or Church yard ...'.[3] The order, in literal albeit tardy compliance with Archbishop of York Grindal's 1571 West Riding injunction below, clearly takes no issue either with the fact of a Summer Lord or with the three Boroughbridge churchwardens' authority to select him.

About 25 July 1592, on a Sunday, 'ther was a Rishbearing at Heptonstall chapell, at what time the yong maides & weomen of the towne of Waddesworth brought burdens of Rishes deckd with flowers to Heptonstall Chapell & with them came a great number of people into the same Chapell ...'. The problem, again, is not with the rushbearing itself but with William Greenwood, a nine- or ten-year-old boy who tried 'to thrust into the Chapell amongst the rest' -- maids, women and young *men*.[4] The cause paper is an assault charge against Henry Crabtree for delivering a sound cuff to wee William's head, not an indictment of rush-bearing. As late as July 1620, Sir Henry Slingsby of Red House contributes 10s 'to give to the younge folkes of Screvine [Scriven] towardes their Reishbearringe' and 12d 'To the boy at his goinge to knarsborough to a Rishbearinge'.[5]

The Doncaster records contain fairly regular entries for maintaining its Maypoles with no noted disturbances at whatever activities were connected with them. In 1578 the Council took them down in timely fashion on 22 July; by 1615 one pole seems to have had a 'seate' connected to it, and by 1632 it may have been alternatively called 'a somertree'.[6] Indeed, such activities met with even the king's approval, as a 1633 London correspondent notes to a West Riding gentry: 'Ther is allso a declaration in print by his maiesties Commandment in fauor of wakes and may-poles, which is as hardly digested by the Puritans, as the putting downe of lectures ...'.[7]

Seldom, however, were sixteenth-century parish entertainments marked by their orderliness -- thus their survival in the records. A 1571 West Riding injunction by Archbishop of York Grindal is quite clear, that the

> minister and churchewardens shall not suffer anye lordes of misrule or sommer lordes, or ladyes or anye disguised persons or others in christmasse or at maye gammes or any minstrels morice daunceres or others at Rishebearinges or at anye other tymes to come vnreverentlye into anye churche or chappell or churcheyeard and there daunce or playe anye vnseemelye partes with scoffes ieastes wanton gestures or rybaulde talke namelye in the tyme of divine service or of anye sermon.[8]

By 1612 the order no longer is news:

> Whereas diuers orders hath beene anciently established in this Court for the suppressing of wakes feasts garries [noisy gatherings] helpales and sundry other such like disordered meetings, heretofore vsed within this westriding aswell vpon the Saboth and holy dayes

as vpon other dayes in the weeke whereunto diuers vagrants persons & men of lewde dispossicion did most vsually resort and there did vse Carding diceing bowling & diuers vnlawfull gaimes whereby in this time of dearth & scarcity there is made vnreasonable wast and Expence of victuall & much excessiue drinking minstrelsie & danceing, Commonly vsed of purpose to draw greate Concourse of people together whereupon did usually follow feighting quarrelling & diuers other disorders to the breach of his Maiesties peace the greate disoner of God & the profamacion of the Lords Day, for Reformacion and suppresseing whereof. It is Orddered by this Court that from henceforth there shall not be any more such wakes feastes garries helpales or assemblies vsed or kept within this Westridding neither shall any faire or Marketts be kept vpon any saboth day within this Westridding ...[9]

Cause for concern is easy to construe. In 1590 Aldborough, Henry Robinson and Wilfrid Ingland were cited 'for behaving them selfes disorderlie in church in service time, in piping dauncing & playing[,] Mr Hudesley the vicar being then preaching'; their performance was assisted by Simon Condall 'who plaid the foole the same time in a fowles Coat'.[10] The Reverend Hudesley -- or perhaps his successor -- suffered further outrage on 14 July 1594 when, following an apparently orderly rushbearing, he

dyd reproue certayne disgised persons that were comed into the churche, & wylled them to come in more humble & reuerent maner to the place, Robert Rodes alias Scotson beyng in the Ale house & vnderstandinge of it, hiered a gonne of Richard Santon of Burrobridge, & gaue him ij d to haue a shott, & comyng onto the churche, so sone as euer the minister had ended his sermond, & before he stirred his fote, on the fore sayd Robert Scotson discharged his gonne, amyng directly ouer the minister, eyther to hit him, as it was reported, or to afray him, & in deed the paper where with the gonne was ramed, light very nighe him, whene he was comed out of the pulpit.[11]

By 1596 it is apparent that the Riding had gone off the rails: Archbishop of York Matthew Hutton's tone is decidedly shrill. Beginning with three reminders 'that no rishbearinges sommer games, morresse daunces, playes enterludes, disguisinges showes, or abuses should be vsed sett fourthe or practised in anye Churche or Churchyearde or vpon the Sabaothe daye or other festivall dayes to the dishonor of god or to the evill example to others or to the hinderance of devyne service or profanation of the Sabbaothe or festivall dayes', he goes on to catalogue the specific abuses of the Cawthorne parishioners, that

> the premisses notwithstandinge the saide defendentes procured the Eveninge prayer vpon Sondaye beinge the xxijth of Auguste 1596. to be sayde oute of due tyme & season that is to saye before the vsuall & accustomed tyme wherein the same was & is vsed to be saide to the ende & purpose that they mighte have the more libertye & space to profane the residue of the saide daye in vngodlye exercyses & pastimes, insolente & lascivious behavioures. And had before purposed resolved & prepared to bestowe the residue of the saide Sabbaothe in suche profane & lewde sportes. And to dresse themselfes in the Church or Chappell of Cawthorne. And in verye deede with the helpe counsell consente & presence of Mary Mountney the wyfe of Thomas Mountney gentleman, did assemble themselves together in the said Churche or Chappell of Cawthorne the Sondaye aforesaide. And there did arme & disguyse themselves some of them putting on womens apparell, other some of them puttinge on longe haire & visardes, & others arminge them with the furnyture of Souldiers, & beinge there thus armed, & disguised, did that daye goe from the Churche, & so wente vp & downe the towne showinge themselves drawinge the people to concourses with them & after them, & shott of guns And when they had spente an houre ij or iij in goinge vp & downe the towne they returned againe into the saide Churche or Chappell of Gawthorpe, And there putt of theire apparell & furniture, & there of committed muche other disorder & abuse to the greefe of the godlye, the danger of their owne soules the contemptes of the Lawes & goode orders aforesaide & to the moste pernicious example to others to offende in the lyke ...

Worse, Hutton had discovered

> that in the monethe of Maye Iune or Iulye 1596 the saide defendantes did procure make or was presente at or consentinge to a rishbear-

inge made & had within the said parishe or Chappell of Cawthorne
vpon a Sabbaothe daye, & made towers, garlandes & other formes of
thinges covered with flowers or procured suche to be made, & carryed or procured to be carryed the same into the saide Churche or
Chappell of Gawthorne, & then sett them vp or procured them to be
sett vp or consented therevnto beinge broughte into the said Churche
or Chappell when the minister was readye to go to prayers, whereby
he was forced to staye the prayers till they had sett vp theire thinges
to the hinderance of devyne service, the breache of the saide godlye
orders, & to the evill example to others to offende in the lyke.[12]

Such riotous behavior was not limited to summertime, of course.
Although Christmas, Hogmanay and Plowdays started off decor-
ously enough according to the Selby Abbey accounts[13], by 1548
the Deanery of Doncaster sputters that

foreasmuch as dronkennes, Idlenes, brawles, dissen<..> & many other
inconvenyences do chaunce betwene neigh<....> neygbor, by thassem-
blie of peple together at wakes & on ploghmundays, it is therfore ordered & enioyned, that hereafter the peple shall vse make or observe
no mo su<..> Wakes ploughmundays or drawynges of the same,
with any assemblie or rowte of peple or otherwise as hath ben<.>
accustomed, vpon payne of forfaytying xls to the kinges highnes for
euery defalte, to be paid by the owner of the plough & householder
wherunto the said plough is Drawne or Wakes is kep<..> ...[14]

A most peculiar aberration, apparently at this time of year and apparently unique to Yorkshire, is the Flower of the Well. At Aldborough on 6 January 1594/5 and at Hunsingore on 14 January
1597/8, divine services were disrupted by men bearing the Flower
of the Well. The Aldborough account is the fuller:

hauyng folowed theire Vanitie althe night in sekynge there Mammet
commonly caled the floure of thwell, [ten named men 'and others']
would nedes bringe the same on a barrow into the churche in prayer
time, and althoughe they were admonished by one of the churche
wardons bothe before & when they came to the churche style, for to
leaue of theyre enterprise & not to trouble the congregation, yet they
would not, but proceded forward with suche a noyse of pyping,

blowyng of an horne, ringyng or strikinge of basons, & showtinge of people *that* the minister was constreyned to leaue of readinge of prayer, yea it was such disorder *that* Mr Raufe Ellicar beyng a stranger merueled att it, & spoke him selfe to *the* churchwardens *that* they should stay it, where vpon the other churche wardon & *the* Cunstable went forthe: And althoughe by them they were stayed from com*m*yng into the churche, yet they continewed the same tumult in the churche yeard for *the* space of a quarter of an hore to the great disquietting bothe of *the* minister & people.[15]

In Hunsingore 'Francis Thompson and George Allen ... did in most contemptious Manner bring into Hunsingore Church a "Toie" called the Flower of the Well in the time of Divine Service', for which entertainment they were stripped naked from the waist up and whipped through the town of Weatherby.[16]

If these two instances are representative, Flower of the Well activities occur around Twelfth Night or Plow Monday -- which in Yorkshire would seem to eliminate flowers as having much to do with it -- and were somehow considered irreligious. 'Mammet' or 'maumet' is an archaic dialect term derived from 'Mohamet', meaning a pagan idol, whether the vaguely medieval sense of 'Mahowne' from the drama[17] or the specific Elizabethan sense of a Roman Catholic saint's image: the *Oxford English Dictionary* is singularly unhelpful in citing for 'definition' the Aldborough example as printed in the *Yorkshire Archaeological Journal*. Given the nature of the West Riding's recusant and Puritan struggles, one might here assume that the Flower of the Well was a Catholic image (or an anti-Protestant image) of sufficient size to be transported to the church in a barrow.

West Riding parishioners were not always left to their own invention of folk activities: helpful vicars dot the cause paper landscape. In 1312 Sherburn-in-Elmet vicar Nicholas de Erghes ran seriously amok, according to ecclesiastical record drawing his parishioners into such extravagences of fornication, incontinence, tavern habitation, and *ludis teatralibus* as have seldom been seen since in Sherburn. William Pistor, chaplain of Ripon Minster in

1312, apparently a year of unreliable clerical vintage, distinguished himself in similar manner.[18] Ripon seems to have been the St. Johns Woods -- or Bethnel Green -- of the West Riding. In 1567 Moor Monkton's Church of All Saints' clerk John Birkbie was found to be

> of verie dissolute lieffe and lewde Conversacion and vsethe veine vndecent apparell namelie great britcheis cut and drawen oute with sarcenet and taffitie, and great Ruffes laid on with laceis of gold and silk and of late toke vpon him to minister or saie devine Service in the Churche of Rippon vpon a holie daie in the assemblie of the people in his Cote without gowne or Cloke with a long sword by his side And he is also vehementlie Suspected to be a notable fforni-cator, and he haithe divers times in the night time bene taken abroade in the towne of Rippon by the wakeman and other officers with Lewde women. and he vseth to Daunce verie offencivelie at alehows-es and mariages in the presence of Common people to the verie evell example of others and the greate Slaunder of the ministerie ...[19]

John Birkbie pales in comparison to Sir Tristram Tyldesley, vicar of Rufforth and Marston,

> who in the yeres of our Lord god 1577 1578 1579 1580 & 1581 or some one or other of the said yeres not having the feare of god be-fore his eyes very vnmodestlye and to the great sclaunder of the ministrye once twice iij iiij^{or} v vj vij viij ix x xj or xij tymes euerye of the said yeres vpon sondais or hollidais hath daunced emongest light youthfull companie both men & women at wed-dinges drynkinges & Rishbearinges or wedding drinking or Rish-bearing in the parishe of Rufforth & the parishe of marstone & other parishes theraboutes & especiallie vpon one sonday or holli-da<y> within one of the said yeres in his dauncing or after wanton-lye & dissolutelye he kissed a mayd or yong woman then a dauncer in his companie, wherat diuers persons were offended & so sore greved that ther was wepons drawne & great dissention arose or was lyke to aryse thervpon to the great disquietnes of godes peace & the Quene maiesties to the great peril & daunger of his soull & to the great sclaunder & offence of a multitude then present & to the perni-cious & wicked example especiallye of yong people then & ther as-

sembled together ... wher vpon a sonday or holliday within the said
tyme he did not onely permit & suffer a Rishbearing within the
church & churchyard of Rufforth wherat was vsed much lewde light
& vnsemelye dauncinges & gestures very vnfit for thes places but
also he hym selve at the said Rishbearing very vnsemelye did Daunce
skip leape & hoighe gallantlye as he thought in his owne folishe &
lewde concepte in the said churchyard emongest a great multituld of
people wher he was derided flowted & laughed at toe the great
sclaunder of the ministry ... [M]any others inhabytantes of Rufforde
and other places theraboutes [say] that Trystrame Tyldesley articu-
lato hath bene a lusty dauncinge prest and offensyve to many both
by his dauncinge and swashing in apparell, not minister lyke.[20]

The unofficial standard of Misrule established by Sir Tristram
may be difficult to surpass, but the West Riding populace of
course gives it a go. Boy Bishops lord it in the Riding from 1315
through 1533, puerile prelates from York, Ripon and Rotherham.
Oddly, Selby records do not suggest that the Abbey had its own
Boy Bishop, although it contributed politicly large sums to
York's, but it did have a King of the Kitchen Boys, documented in
1416, 1431 and 1483.[21] I can find no explanation of the King of
the Kitchen Boys' functions, although it does not take a great
stretch of domestic imagination to supply that want. Sir Arthur Ingram of Sheriff Hutton, Temple Newsam and York seems to have
continued the Riding tradition of a 'King in the Kitchin', who received a 5s reward in 1637.[22]

More peculiar as a Lord of Misrule is Guisborough's version,
documented in a 4 March 1636/7 letter from one Richard Wynne
to Thomas Wentworth, then in Ireland. Omitting the correspondent's rather cringing tone to Wentworth, which is not explained
by the content of the letter, one learns of 'a leuity of cutting of
hatts ... at Gisborough about the middle of September last':

The occasion of that meting was, a leaue-taking betwene Mr Foulis
& Mr Chaloner, to which purpose, bycause Mr Chaloner could not
goe to Ingelby, being to returne another way, he invited Mr Foulis &
his brethren to dinner to the taverne at Gisborough. Four of them

came, and my self amongst other tenants to Mr Chaloner & some strangers was also invited. There were at dinner to the number of 15 as I remember. After dinner (the number then being aboue 20) they fell vpon the said leuity; But that there was anie such health as your Lordship hath beene informed of or anie thing tending that way, as I desire to haue credit with your Lordship in anie thing or reputacion amongst honest men, there was no such matter to my knowledge or observacion, neither to my very best remembrance was your Lordship so much as named by anie man in that companie that day, that which was, being onlie a meere and casuall merriment helped on by the presence of one who is a merrie companion and personated a knight Errant or a kinde of Lord of Misrule amongst them. And for Mr Chaloner, whose departure out of the Countrey begott this meting, my opinion of him is that hee is a verie abill & modest gentleman and as inoffensiue in his deportment & behaviour as anie man I haue beene acquainted & accompanied withall.[23]

Attempts to define this 'cutting of hats' form of misrule through standard folk custom and antiquarian sources have been unsuccessful.

Thus the West Riding parishes danced and marched to their own drummers, pipers and vicars; what survives in the folk records includes rushbearings, summer games, Maypoles, various Lords of Misrule from Boy Bishop to Kitchen King to the Cutting of Hats, the Flower of the Well, parish plays and household masques not noted here, and processional parish dances complete with costumes and kissing. Almost all extant accounts seem to have involved some sort of disguising, some sort of mimetic or parodic activity and some sort of brush with authority, frequently because that authority served as the object of the parody. Plainly evident from the surviving records, however, is the extent to which this county's parish entertainment activities mirror its political, social and religious tensions. Controversies between Royalist and Parliamentarian, Puritan and Anglican, Anglican and recusant, gentry and commoner seem to simmer in these parish communities over the years, boiling over in the extant entertainment records which describe the discord.

Notes

1   Borthwick Institute, York, MS. CP.f.246, sheets 1-2. The examination took place on 23 January 1469/70 following the Summer Game held on 18 June 1469.

2   My thanks for the English translations are due to Dr. Abigail A. Young, Research Associate at the Records of Early English Drama, University of Toronto. Appreciation also is due to the United States National Endowment for the Humanities, who funded the collection of these records for the West Riding, Yorkshire Records of Early English Drama project; and to the gracious, knowledgeable English archival staffs without whom the West Riding collection could not have been accomplished.

3   Chester County Record Office, Diocesan Visitation EDV 1/8b, 14 November 1589. Transcriptions from the records in this present article silently omit irrelevant words or letters canceled by the scribe; silently incorporate the clerk's interlinear corrections; mark manuscript deterioration by ellipses within diamond brackets -- e.g., <...>; and record this author's editorial clarifications within square brackets.

4   Borthwick Institute, York, MS. CP.g.2651, fol. 1.

5   Yorkshire Archaeological Society, Leeds, MS. DD56/J/3/4, fol. 98 (8 July 1620) and fol. 99v (20 July 1620).

6   Doncaster Archives, MS. AB.2/1/1, fol. 103 ('mawdlayns' fair: 22 July 1578); MS. AB.6/1/2/3, p. 16 (March 1615/16); and MS. AB.6/1/2/8, fol. 4v (27 October 1632). An additional 11 November 1629 (or 1630) payment 'to ffrancis Ward for mending the suer at Robart Palmer house noake and about the mapoull and for stoufe for it vj s. vj d.' also survives in MS. AB.6/1/2/7, p. 10.

7   Sheffield City Archives, MS. WWM/STR P 13/79, fols. 2-3 (29 October 1633); from Lord Cottington at Charing Cross to Thomas Wentworth, Earl of Strafford, then either at Wentworth Woodhouse, West Riding, or else in Ireland.

8   Borthwick Institute, York, Injunctions to the Laity of Archbishop Grindal, Archbishop's Register 30, fol. 130v.

9   Yorkshire Archaeological Society, MS. Fairfax M38, fols. 135-36 (20 April 1612, Quarter Sessions at Pontefract).

10 Borthwick Institute, York, V.1590-1/CB.2, fol. 22v.

11 Borthwick Institute, York, H.C.CP.N.D./11, fol. 1.

12 Borthwick Institute, York, HC.CP.1596/7, fols. 1-2.

13 Hull University Library, MSS. DDLO(2)8/6, fol. 8 (1522/23) and DDLO/2/8/9, fol. 3v; both record payments to the plow boys for Plowday. Hogmanay, 31 December, also was observed by Selby Abbey.

14 Sheffield City Archives, MS. Bacon-Frank 11-3, fol. 3.

15 Borthwick Institute, York, H.C.CP.N.D./11, fol. 1. HCCP/N.D./11 is not dated by year, but within the appropriate time span only in 1594–95 does Sunday fall on both 14 July and 6 January, Epiphany Sunday.

16 York Minster Library, Hailstone MS. BB 52, fol. 8. The original 1597/98 West Riding Sessions Roll has disappeared since Edward Hailstone made his copy on 30 April 1884.

17 See, for example, the Towneley Cycle's *Magnus Herodes* pageant, where Herod's association with 'Mahowne' -- swearing by Mahowne, cousin to Mahowne, protected by Mahowne -- is almost a generic pagan link; as A. C. Cawley (*The Wakefield Pageants in the Towneley Cycle*, Manchester, University of Manchester Press, 1958, p. 114) notes, 'Mahowne' or 'Mahomet' is 'represented as a heathen deity scarcely distinguishable from the devil' both here and in the York Cycle.

18 Borthwick Institute, York, Register Vol. 8, fol. 5 (17 August 1312) for the Sherburn-in-Elmet case and the same Register, fols. 8 and 218 (15 September, 17 October) for the Ripon disturbances.

19 Borthwick Institute, York, V.1567-8, fols. 104v-105.

20 Borthwick Institute, York, C.P.G.3306, fols. 1-5.

21 The Selby Abbey records are catalogued as MSS. DD LO/20 at the University of Hull and as Se/Ac at Westminster Diocesan Archives, London.

22 Leeds City Archives, Sheepscar, MS. TN/EA/13/23, fol. 22v.

23 Sheffield City Archives, MS. WWM/STR P 16/144, fol. 1v (4 March 1636/7), letter from Richard Wynne to Wentworth. Guisborough and Ingleby are in the North Riding of Yorkshire, whereas Wentworth's properties and tenants were based largely in the West Riding. The 'cutting of hats' may be a peculiar form of North Riding misrule.

'What Revels are in Hand?'
Dramatic Activities Sponsored by the Parishes
of the Thames Valley

Alexandra F. Johnston

The Thames Valley above London provides us with a particularly full and useful collection of evidence that illustrates the variety of activities that are recorded in other English counties. We have manuscript evidence from eighty parishes -- thirty-four from Berkshire, thirteen from Buckinghamshire and thirty-three from Oxfordshire along with the accounts from Kingston-upon-Thames and Guildford in Surrey and a few stray parishes in rural Middlesex. We are also blessed in the Thames Valley counties by having rich, discursive and early accounts from four substantial parishes -- All Saints' Kingston, St. Laurence' Reading, St. Mary's Henley and St. Mary's Thame which, like Reading in our period, is on a tributary of the Thames not on the river itself. The evidence surviving in all these accounts is of three kinds -- churchwardens' accounts, prosecutions before the ecclesiastical courts and the occasional reference to events in another parish in a set of churchwardens' accounts. What it documents is four specific types of parish dramatic activity -- the folk play, the Biblical play, plays on other themes and what may be a variant on all of these types, the itinerant parish play.

The Folk Play[1]
We have evidence for King Games or ceremonies involving summer lords and ladies from twelve parishes. The earliest is from Henley in 1454–55 and the latest from Burford on the other side of Oxfordsire in 1630–31. The evidence records five distinguish-

able activities -- the custom of a summer lord, or lord and lady, Robin Hood with his followers, morris dancers, maypoles, and some activity that demanded a bower. The truly tangled part of the puzzle presented by the laconic evidence is the relationship between the figure of the summer lord and Robin Hood. Although I once believed that the figure of Robin Hood could take the place of a summer lord[2], I no longer believe that this is so. Rather, it seems we have two kinds of figures represented here. At the summer festivals in some locations it seems to have been the custom to elect members of the community to be "king" or "queen" for however long the festivities lasted. These individuals presided over the many activities that were included in the summer customs of that location. It seems clear that these figure were not Bakhtinian subversive figures. Because they operated, like the Boy Bishops, in a situation of licensed liberty, they were figures that reinforced the established social order rather than subverting it. Sometimes the summer lords were young men of the parish, as in Henley in 1502, when Richard Andrew, son of John Andrew, dyer, was named the lord.[3] Sometimes servants of the local gentry presided over the events. We have a decade a half of evidence from Wing in Buckinghamshire where the king and queen are named in the records and the names of their masters are also provided.[4] This was a conscious inversion of order, a custom that placed a "non-elite" member of the community in the position of control to preside over the summer festival. The chosen ruler was, as Shakespeare tells us, in *Winter's Tale*, to

> ... bid
> These unknown friends to's welcome; for it is
> A way to make us better friends, more known ...[5]

This figure was often provided with a bower that served as a focal point of the festivities and was crowned, as Perdita is in *Winter's Tale*, with garlands. This is a figure of order, of reconciliation, not of disorder.

And here the problem with the identification of Robin Hood with the summer lord becomes apparent. However fragmentary and elusive the evidence, the Robin Hood of legend and poem is an outlaw, a disturber of the peace, a figure of energy and combat. As such, the Robin Hood figures provide the counterpoint of disorder to the order of the summer lords. The lords presided but Robin Hood gathered money. Robin Hood and his "fellows" -- named frequently as Little John in Kingston in the early sixteenth century and again in Woodstock more than a century later[6] -- regularly transmitted money that they had "gathered" to the churchwardens. To gather the money, they could have been engaged in any one of three activities. First, they may simply have swaggered about playing the part of the outlaws of the legend demanding payment in a form of mock extortion. Secondly, they may have teamed up with the morris dancers for a mimetic event. The sixteenth-century text of Robin Hood and the Friar may represent this possibility. The surviving text fits well with a situation where the two parish troupes -- Robin Hood and his company and the morris dancers possibly led by the friar figure -- come together for a farce full of horseplay and violence that ends with a dance.[7] A third variant that fits the evidence of the other surviving fragment of text 'Robin Hood and the Potter' and many of the nondramatic "gests" is, of course, the combat game. This was probably a sporting contest -- a wrestling match or an archery contest or a fight with staves or any other variant on the contest theme. Late evidence from Witney in the 1620s has the summer festivals called 'Whitson sports'.[8] Witney is not far from the Gloucestershire border where a decade later Robert Dover staged his famous Cotswold Games.

The evidence for folk drama from the Thames Valley parishes, then, is for two separate "games" co-existing within the same festive season -- the election or appointment of a mock ruler to preside over the "king game" and the more boisterous figures of Robin Hood and his troupe who were sometimes, in some way, attached to the mock court.

Biblical Plays

The dominance of the so-called "cycle plays" in our thinking about Biblical plays is perpetuated in the title of Norman Davis' Early English Text Society volume *Non-Cycle Plays and Fragments*.[9] In that volume we have the texts of the Brome Abraham and the Northampton Abraham. These two plays represent what is emerging as an important element in parish drama. In St. Laurence' Reading and in St. Mary's Thame we have records that, though laconic, are detailed enough to give us some idea of the setting of these plays. The earliest single episode Biblical play is the play of Jacob and his twelve Sons in Thame in 1481.[10] Reading St. Laurence had a Creation play in 1506–07[11] and a play that included Cain in 1511–12 and again in 1515–16.[12] These Reading plays were played on a trestle stage built against the wall of the Benedictine Abbey in a space called the Forbury. Although the profits were not as large as those made at the midsummer "gatherings", the parish coffers did benefit from the plays. Both parishes also performed plays on the Kings of Cologne -- on May Day in Reading in 1499[13] and on Corpus Christi in Thame in 1522.[14] There is no way for us to determine how many of the innumerable anonymous "plays" recorded in other parish documents are single Biblical episodes and how many are folk plays. However, the evidence of named plays from the Thames Valley is important since it provides a setting for the single episode plays that have survived both in single manuscripts such as the Brome and Northampton Abrahams and in manuscripts that seem to represent anthologies of Biblical plays the Towneley and N-Town manuscripts.

A second genre of Biblical plays performed by the parishes of the Thames Valley are Easter plays. Each of the four major parishes -- All Saints' Kingston, St. Laurence' Reading, St. Mary's Henley, and St. Mary's Thame -- record the regular performances of Easter plays. There is always the possibility when a parish document speaks of an Easter dramatic event that what is being documented is a dramatic embellishment of the liturgy and not true drama. However, the St. Laurence accounts record a payment for the writing of a playbook by Mr Laborne the chantry priest[15] and there are similar records in Thame[16] and Henley.[17] When similar evidence found by Sally-Beth MacLean in Kingston-upon-Thames[18] is added, a clear pattern emerges. As far as we can tell from the laconic entries, what went on in these parishes around Easter was close to what is recorded in Bodleian MS E Museo -- the text that appears in the Early English Text Society *Digby Plays* as Christ's Burial and Resurrection.[19] From a rubric in the manuscript, we are told that the first part of the story -- up to the deposition and burial -- was portrayed on Good Friday while the Resurrection sequence took place on Easter afternoon or on Easter Monday. On the face of it, it would be nice to claim the Bodley MS as the Thames Valley play but it has been identified from its dialect as a northern text and, therefore, it is unlikely to be the text used in the Thames Valley. The records and the manuscript seem to represent the same tradition in widely separated parts of the country. James Gibson has collected extensive evidence of a Passion Play at New Romney in Kent.[20] Other evidence of Easter plays survive from sources as diverse as the "Shrewsbury Fragments"[21] and the plays of John Bale.[22] Indeed a case can be made that, as in France, the most common kind of Biblical play in England was some form of Easter play. The evidence from the Thames Valley is an important part of the argument.[23] What is clear is that small scale Biblical drama was far more common than the ambitious processional plays of the midland and northern cities. Our understanding of the genre of early drama in Engand has been badly skewed by the survival of play texts. The busy antiquarians of East Anglia, Chester, and the West Riding of Yorkshire and the hard-headed city council of York preserved plays for reasons we can only guess at. As the critical mass of record evidence grows, bringing us more insights into playmaking in the period we should turn again to the manuscript "fragments" we have neglected to see if, like the E Museo MS, they may represent an important but neglected element of early drama.

Plays on other themes

There are four other references in the Thames Valley material to dramatic activity that are neither folk plays nor on Biblical themes. Two come from Thame. One records a St. George play in 1482–83[24] and a second is the mysterious entry for 1488–89 recording one penny 'in expensis quando le box ludi ffabine & sabine'.[25] Whether this is evidence of a regular play on the lives of Saints Fabinus and Sabinus or whether this is a record of a puppet play is impossible to determine. A court record tells of us a 'godly interlude' played in the church at Winslow in Buckinghamshire in 1580[26] and in 1593–94 the parish of Great Marlowe had a play in the church loft.[27] These last two references may be to Biblical drama. They are important because of their late dates and because both were apparently played in the church providing further evidence that churches remained important playing venus well after the Reformation.

Itinerant Parish Plays

Finally, the Thames Valley counties provide considerable evidence for the phenomenon of travelling parish troupes. Sally-Beth Mac-Lean has argued that the summer king from Kingston went in mock progress by barge from Kingston to the small villages that comprised Kingston's "hinterland" in emulation of the progresses along the river of the real king from his palace at Richmond across the river.[28] In the Kingston records there are expences incurred for a parish "king game" visit to such tiny villages as Teddington, Long Ditton, West Mulsey, Hampton, Walton, Croydon, and Cheam all in the first few decades of the sixteenth century. Such visitations sometimes included the whole mock court, but, in 1505–06, from Reading St. Laurence, we have evidence of a supper provided for only 'Robynhod & his company when he came from ffynchamsted'.[29]

A variant on the travelling game seems to have been an itinerant Robin Hood and his company who actually gathered money for their home parish. Among the Kingston receipts for 1513–14 we find an entry recording money gathered by Robin Hood at the neighbouring town of Croydon.[30] Similarly, in 1504–05, Henley held their regular king game but it was their visiting Robin Hood figures who were paid by Reading St. Laurence in that same year.[31] This custom of touring Robin Hoods may explain the laconic payments in the accounts of the Reading Guild Merchant for the years between 1382 and 1428 when payments are made to 'players' from the villages of Aldermaston, Wokingham, Sindlesham, Yately in Hampshire and Henley in Oxfordshire.[32]

The players also visited schools and monastic houses. The Provost of Eton paid players from Uxbridge in Middlesex in 1486–87[33] and the prior of Bicester priory in Oxfordshire paid half a mark to the 'lusoribus' of Bicester to perform a play on Amys and Amylon in 1424.[34]

There were also troupes of parish players who appear in private accounts and in the accounts of other incorporated towns who are named as coming from a town or parish. Sir Edward Don the Sheriff of Buckingham for most of the first half of the sixteenth century paid the players of Windsor at Christmas 1532[35] and those of Watlington at Christmas 1537[36] to play in his hall at Saunderton. In 1555–56, Banbury in Oxfordshire paid players from Bramley.[37]

This pattern of itinerant players is common all over the country and is one of the most intriguing and unexpected results of the work of the Records of Early English Drama project. These are not the retained players of great magnates or even of lesser ones. Nor are they the players of large centres such as Coventry whose core of professional players were familiar figures on the roads of Warwickshire, Oxfordshire, and Gloucestershire.[38] Rather these were apparently local talent earning money for the parish by providing entertainment for the local dignitary.

And this last point is the telling one. Parish drama in its many forms was a money-making venture that allowed the churchwardens to keep the fabric of their ancient churches together. Whatever other functions this playmaking served -- to build community, to celebrate the seasons, or to teach the parishioners the stories of the faith, it was nevertheless a fundamental part of the economy of every parish.

Notes

1 I have treated this subject at greater length in "Summer Festivals in the Thames Valley Counties", Thomas Pettitt and Leif Søndergaard [eds.], *Custom, Culture and Community*, Odense, 1994, pp. 37-56.

2 Alexandra F. Johnston, "English Puritanism and Festive Custom", *Renaissance and Reformation* 15 [NS] (1991), p. 293.

3 Oxfordshire Record Office, MSS DD Henley A V/3, fol. 6v.

4 Buckinghamshire Record Office, PR 234/5/1, fols. 67v-80.

5 Shakespeare, *The Winter's Tale*, IV, iv, ll. 64-66.

6 Oxfordshire Record Office, MSS DD Par. Woodstock c. 12, p. 17.

7 Mary A. Blackstone [ed.], *Robin Hood and the Friar*, Toronto, 1981 (PLS Performance Texts, 3).

8 Oxfordshire Record Office, MSS DD Par. Witney c. 9, fols. 43 and 49v.

9 Norman Davis [ed.], *Non-cycle Plays and Fragments*, Oxford and London, Oxford University Press, 1970 (Early English Text Society, Supplementary Series, 1).

10 Oxfordshire Record Office, MSS DD Par. Thame, b. 2, fol. 41v.

11 Berkshire Record Office, D/P 97 5/1, p. 31.

12 Berkshire Record Office, D/P 97 5/1, pp. 88 and 106.

13 Berkshire Record Office, D/P 97 5/1, p. 3.

14 Oxfordshire Record Office, MSS DD Par. Thame c. 5, fol. 76v.

15 Berkshire Record Office, D/P 97 5/1, pp. 194 and 202.

16 Oxfordshire Record Office, MSS DD Par. Thame b. 2, fol. 73v *et passim*.

17 Oxfordshire Record Office, MSS DD Henley A V/3, fol. 27v. *et passim*.

18 Surrey Record Office, KG 2/2/1, p. 99 *et passim*.

19 F. J. Furnivall [ed.], *The Digby Plays*, London, Oxford University Press, 1896 (Early English Text Society, Extra Series, 70).

20 See his article "'Interludum Passionis Domini': Parish Drama in Medieval New Romney", in this collection, pp. 139-50.

21 Ian Lancashire, *Dramatic Texts and Records of Britain*, Toronto, University of Toronto Press, 1984, p. 843.

22 Lancashire, *Dramatic Texts*, p. 282.

23 Alexandra F. Johnston, "The Continental Connection: A Reconsidera-

tion", Robert W. Frank and Alan Knight [eds.], *The Stage as Mirror: Civic Theatre in Late Medieval Europe*, London, Boydell & Brewer (forthcoming).

24 Oxfordshire Record Office, MSS DD Par. Thame c. 5, fol. 42.

25 Oxfordshire Record Office, MSS DD Par. Thame c. 5, fol. 44v.

26 Hertfordshire Record Office, ASA 7/17, fol. 277v.

27 Buckinghamshire Record Office, PR 140 5/1, fol. 4.

28 Sally-Beth MacLean, "King Games and Robin Hood: Play and Profit at Kingston upon Thames", Jean-Claude Aubailly and Edelgard E. DuBruck [eds.], *Le Théâtre et la Cité dans l'Europe médiévale*, Stuttgart, Hans-Dieter Heinz Akademischer Verlag, 1988, p. 309 [*Fifteenth-Century Studies*, 13 (1988)].

29 Berkshire Record Office, D/P 97 5/1, p. 25.

30 Surrey Record Office, KG 2/2/1, p. 74.

31 Berkshire Record Office, D/P 97 5/1, p. 21.

32 Until dissolution, the Benedictine Abbey was the overlord of the town of Reading and the abbot confirmed the master of the Guild Merchant as the chief burgess every year. Reading was incorporated in 1542. The town accounts before 1542 are in fact the accounts of the Guild Merchant. The early accounts were destroyed by enemy action during the Second World War but they were transcribed for the Historical Manuscript Commission for the 11th Report. For the accounts for 1382–86, see W. D. Macray [ed.], "The Manuscripts of the Corporation of Reading", 11th Report, Appendix 7, p. 172. Macray also supplies some readings now obliterated in Berkshire RO R/FCa 2/1-11 (1413–21) for 1413–14 and 1419–20. The evidence for 1423–24 is found in R/FCa 2/12-32.

33 Eton College, Audit Roll AR/F/2, mb. 3.

34 Alexandra F. Johnston, "Amys and Amylon in Bicester Priory", *REED Newsletter* 18 (1993), pp. 15-18.

35 Warwickshire Record Office, CR 895/106, fol. 200.

36 Warwickshire Record Office, CR 895/106, fol. 235v.

37 Oxfordshire Record Office, BB XVII i/1, fol. 170v.

38 The players of Coventry are particularly prominent being frequent visitors to nearby Maxstoke Priory in the fifteenth century (see Trinity College Oxford, MS. TRIN. COLL. C. 84 now deposited in the Bodleian), playing for Prior More in 1528 (D. N. Klausner, *Records of Early English Drama* [hereafter *REED*]: *Herefordshire / Worcestershire*, Toronto, University of Toronto Press, 1990, p. 501) and being paid by the corporation of Coventry itself in 1590 (R. W. Ingram [ed.], *REED: Coventry*, Toronto, University of Toronto Press, 1990, p. 328). Players from Slimbridge and Wooton-under-edge in Gloucestershire performed for Richard

Beauchamp, Earl of Warwick at Longleat (Audrey Douglas and Peter Greenfield [eds.], REED: *Cumberland / Westmorland and Gloucester- shire*, Toronto, University of Toronto Press, 1990, p. 347) and village players from the Worcester villages of Cleeve Prior, Martley and Ombers- ley all played for that most generous ecclesiastical patron Prior More of Worcester in the years just before the Reformation (Klausner, *REED: Herefordshire / Worcestershire*, pp. 513, 463 and 529). The Shuttle- worths of Smithills in Lancashire welcomed players from Preston in 1588–89 and Rochdale in 1591 (David George [ed.], *REED: Lan- cashire*, Toronto, University of Toronto Press, 1990, pp. 167-68).

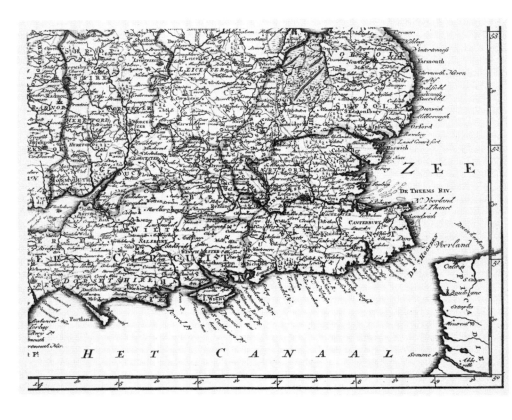

Figure 8:

The Thames Watershed. [From: *Nieuwe en Beknopte Hand-Atlas bestaande in eene Verzameling van eenige der algemeenste en nodigste Landkaarten*, Amsterdam, Isaak Tirion, 1744.]

Parish Drama in Four Counties
Bordering the Thames Watershed

Peter H. Greenfield

By happy accident, my efforts for the Records of Early English Drama series have involved editing the records of four counties adjacent to those discussed by Alexandra Johnston in her article "'What Revels are in Hand: Dramatic Activities Sponsored by the Parishes of the Thames Valley" (this volume, pp. 95-104). Gloucestershire lies to the northwest of the Thames Valley, Hampshire to the south, and Hertfordshire and Bedfordshire to the northeast. If the Thames Valley counties had a relatively unified dramatic tradition because the river linked them, then examining the surrounding counties may provide some indications of the role of topography in the development of different dramatic traditions. The fragmentary evidence from these four counties permits no broad conclusions, but some interesting patterns do emerge.

Gloucestershire would seem to be a promising county for such a topographic study, as it is made up of three distinct regions. The gentle eastern slope of the Cotswolds actually forms the westernmost reach of the Thames watershed, while west of the steep Cotswold Edge runs the Severn valley, and further west the rugged and sparsely populated Forest of Dean. Unfortunately, no records of dramatic activity survive from parishes in either the Cotswolds or the Forest of Dean. Of twenty-six Gloucestershire parishes with churchwardens' accounts dating from before 1642, only eight have accounts from before 1600, and only four of those go back as far as the 1550s. Three of those four come from Gloucester city parishes, the fourth from Minchinhampton, on the western side of the Cotswolds; none of the four contains anything more dramatic than sepulchre-watching.

Indeed, the lone parish offering evidence of dramatic activity in the county is Tewkesbury. The churchwardens' accounts contain fifteen references to renting the 'players geare' between 1567 and 1585. The churchwardens twice inventoried their store of costumes and props during these years, and in 1577–78 paid for additions and renovations to the wardrobe. The renters often came from nearby villages, such as Mathon, eleven miles north in Worcestershire. At least once a parishioner hired the gear, and itinerant players might also have rented it.[1] Presumably the parish used these costumes in its own performances, but the only record that may point to such use over the period when the 'players geare' was rented out is a single payment in 1575–76 for mending a seat broken during a play.[2]

In 1600 the parish put on three plays at Whitsun in order to finance constructing a stone battlement on the church tower to replace the lead spire that had fallen down forty years earlier. The churchwardens decided on a traditional Whitsun-ale, offering the plays in conjunction with selling ale brewed from donated grain. The town council objected, citing customary abuses at such ales, and forced the parish to settle for selling the donated wheat and malt as grain. The council did not object to the plays, however, and permitted them as a means of drawing attention to the grain sale.[3]

The uniqueness of the event can be seen in the fact that the churchwardens separated it from the rest of their accounts for the year. Certainly the expenditures suggest the plays were produced far more lavishly than any had previously been in Tewkesbury. Costumes were hired -- in addition to or in place of the old wardrobe -- and musicians paid to play 'all the tyme'. Further, one 'T. B.' was paid 30s 'for his charges', the size of the sum perhaps indicating that T. B. functioned like the 'property players' mentioned in the records of several East Anglian towns -- professional men of the theatre who organized and directed local amateur performances.[4]

108

According to both the churchwardens' accounts and the minutes of the borough council, 'iij severall stage playes' were performed 'within the abbey'. Taken with the earlier reference to the broken seat, this language may indicate a tradition of performing inside the church itself. If so, the 1600 performance represents a very late instance of playing inside a church.[5] Whether the church or some other site was used, the payment of 13s 4d 'for a place to playe in', must refer to the construction of a stage, since it seems unlikely that the parish would charge itself rent for the use of the church, or any other space 'within the abbey'.

The expenses for constructing the battlement and producing the plays amounted to £66, while the receipts from the sale of grain, from the sale of lead and timber from the old spire, and from the plays came to £45. Although the plays themselves made a negligible profit of 14s 5d, the summary statement at the end of the account says that the £21 deficit represents the difference between what the churchwardens spent and what 'they gained by their playes', the language showing that the plays contributed vitally to the financial success of the whole enterprise.

Though we know far more about the finances of Tewkesbury's parish plays than we do about the plays themselves, two inventories of the players' gear suggest biblical subject matter: entries include 'vj sheepe skyns for Christes garmentes', 'a face or vysor for the devyll' and wigs and beards 'for the apostles'.[6] The dramatic tradition of Tewkesbury, located in the Severn valley, thus has parallels with Thames Valley parishes that put on relatively elaborate biblical plays to raise money -- Kingston, Reading and especially Thame.[7] These parallels do not, of course, necessarily establish any continuity or connections between the two areas. Recent work on the itineraries of professional players suggests that they rarely crossed the Cotswold Hills, which separate the Thames and Severn watersheds, probably because getting a cart loaded with costumes and props up or down the steep Cotswold Edge was a misery they did not need. Instead, they preferred to reach Gloucester, Tewkesbury and Worcester by following the Severn north from Bristol. The Cotswolds could have provided a similar barrier to the spread of parish dramatic traditions.

The geographical connections seem rather more solid when we move southeast to Hampshire. The chances of finding records of parish drama in Hampshire are considerably better than for Gloucestershire, since twenty Hampshire parishes have extant churchwardens' accounts for the period before 1642, eleven dating before 1600, six before 1550, and two before 1500. Eight parishes offer evidence of dramatic activity, and in each case the evidence involves some kind of king game like those frequently found in the Thames Valley just to the north. Since none of the surviving records yield many details about the nature of the celebration, we can only guess that they may have resembled the king games involving Robin Hood held at Kingston and at St. Laurence, Reading.[8]

The earliest reference to a king ale in Hampshire comes from the single parish of Andover borough, which has churchwardens' accounts covering the four years from 1470 to 1474. The 1471–72 accounts include receipts for a king ale from six pairs of people, presumably collectors, and five of those pairs consist of a man and a woman not married to each other. Philip Morant collected 24s with William Sadeler, but 'Philypp Moranttes wiff' (as she is named in the records) collected her 17s 5d with Richard Curtes.[9] This practice seems a relatively innocent one, however, when compared to some of the other activities men and women indulged in at church ales that we have discovered in church court records.

Bramley parish provides more detailed accounts of king ales at Whitsun in 1531 and 1532. In both years the receipts include collections taken at feasts on Whitsunday, Whitmonday, Tuesday and Wednesday, and on Trinity Sunday. Expenses include payments to a minstrel, as well as for considerable quantities of meat and other foodstuffs. Several adjoining parishes participated in the Bramley king ale: the 1531 receipts include contributions from

Pamber and Stratfield Saye; the 1532 receipts, from Silchester and Hartley.[10] The ale appears to have been an annual event at Bramley until the end of the sixteenth century, although the records never again provide so much detail, instead recording only the profit as 'Clere gaynes at Whitsontide'.[11]

Similar but later evidence comes from the parish of Wotton St. Lawrence. Mentions of king ales occur in the accounts for 1567, 1575, 1579, and 1580, but the detailed accounts are those from 1600, 1603, 1605, and 1612, by which time most parishes had either abandoned their king ale entirely, or at least become much cagier about recording its existence. The detailed accounts reveal a festive practice much like Bramley's: the expenses primarily involve costs for food, while the receipts come from gatherings over several days. In 1612 the king ale ran from Whitsunday to Trinity Sunday, just as at Bramley, but in 1600 it took place later in the year and spread over nearly a month. The first gathering was made on the 'sonday senight before midsomer', the second on the Sunday before midsummer, the third on that Monday, the fourth on the Sunday after midsummer (29 June) and the last on the following Sunday (6 July).[12]

The Wotton St. Lawrence records also provide a few hints about the nature of the entertainment associated with all the feasting. Payments to musicians occur in all four sets of detailed accounts, but most interesting are the payments in 1600 for the 'Ladyes Lyueries' and the 'Lordes Lyueries', certainly appropriate costumes for some sort of king game or summer game. The immediately following entry records two shillings paid 'to Whitburne for his play'. That Whitburne was paid for writing a play text seems unlikely, but so does the idea that the churchwardens were underwriting his gambling, which is what 'for his play' so often means in household accounts. Still, there is the puzzling entry in the same year's accounts of 10s 6d received 'for the play at Pewter', which does suggest something like gambling for donated pewter utensils.

The other evidence of king ales in Hampshire is scattered and sketchy. Crondall held ales in the 1540s and the parish morris players performed before the Marquess of Exeter in 1555–56.[13] The Stoke Charity churchwardens' accounts record king ales from 1541 to 1581.[14] Evidence of similar festivity at Newton Valence comes from a 1580 matrimonial case in the consistory court of Winchester diocese, in which one John Smith of Drox-ford admitted he had proposed marriage to Clarice Baker when he 'was somer lord & the said Clarice was sumer lady of newton'.[15] A Star Chamber case concerns what may have been an attempt to revive a king ale tradition at Alton in 1611, when a number of pa-rishioners fell afoul of the constable for dancing in the 'somer howse' to the accompaniment of an itinerant fiddler.[16] Finally, the churchwardens' accounts of South Warnborough for 1611 in-clude payments of 9d for 'Morris bells that were lost' and 16d for 'boordinge of ij minstrells', both of which probably had some-thing to do with a Whitsun ale like that recorded in the 1621 re-ceipts.[17]

Plotting these parishes on a map of the county tempts one to-ward some geographical generalizations. All the parishes mention-ed are in the northern half of the county, north of Winchester. Al-ton, Crondall and Newton Valence actually lie within the Thames watershed, as they are located in the northeastern sector of the county in valleys that drain northeast through Surrey to the Thames. Bramley sits just south of the Hampshire-Berkshire bor-der, nearly atop the divide between the Thames Valley and the Test, Itchen and Meon watersheds, which drain the rest of Hamp-shire into the Solent. Andover and Stoke Charity are in the Test valley, but in its upper reaches, still relatively close to the Berk-shire border. The obvious conclusion would be that the dramatic traditions of the Thames Valley spread south only half the length of Hampshire, but did not penetrate to the coastal plain south of Winchester.

112

This conclusion may be misleading, however, since we lack sufficient evidence from parishes in that southern half of the county. Only three such parishes have extant pre-1642 church-wardens' accounts. Of those, Upham's accounts begin only in 1640, and those of Hambledon begin in 1600 -- early enough to get extensive evidence of king ales at Wotton St. Lawrence, but such late detailed records are of course very unusual. The Fordingbridge records seem more promising, as the parish preserved an unbroken run of churchwardens' accounts from 1490 to 1639, but most of the accounts are summary in form. Among the rare itemized accounts occurs a single reference to an ale in 1519, but whether that ale had any relation to the king ale traditions of parishes to the north is uncertain.

A somewhat more trustworthy geographical distinction emerges when we move northwest to Hertfordshire. The evidence is not extensive -- pre-1600 churchwardens' accounts survive from only eight parishes, and only one of those contains relevant records -- but it does suggest that the western half of the county developed a tradition of parish drama associated with that of the Thames Valley, while the eastern half of the county has more in common with East Anglia.

In 1589, Lord Burghley and the bishop of London examined William Dyke, deacon of St. Michael's parish, St. Albans, about the extreme views expressed in his preaching. Asked about his attacks on the Whitsun ale at nearby Redbourn, Dyke replied:

> I answer that theire Whyttson Ales in their originall beinge badd, and by the marvelous and shameful abuses in them made farre worse, drawing the people of other parishes vnto them from the exercises of gods word which they might haue had at home, and hauing in them pypinge dauncinge, and Maid Marion comyng into the Churche in the time of prayer and preachinge to move laughter with kissinge in the churche besides sondrie other abuses ...[18]

Redbourn is located well to the west of the county, near the Buckinghamshire border. That Robin Hood games were common on that side of the county is reinforced by Francis Taverner's early seventeenth-century history of the village of Hexton, in which Taverner writes of the 'Maying feasts, with their playes of Robynhood, and little Iohn', which Hexton had only recently abandoned.[19]

The parish dramatic traditions of the eastern side of the county emerge from the churchwardens' accounts of Bishop's Stortford. Receipts 'de le pleye' or of 'the playe silver' occur in the accounts for 1490, 1491, 1511–12, 1524–25, and 1532, but it seems likely that the play began much earlier, as the 1482 accounts include expenses for repairing the dragon. The dragon was still around in 1543, when the inventory of church goods listed 'a dragon made of hoopis & couered with canvas'.[20] Moreover, the records suggest that the Stortford play was part of a festive tradition that involved a number of towns and villages in the area, for in 1503 the churchwardens received 4d 'of the dragvn to brawyng playe', while in 1540 they spent money 'at stansted playe'. They also paid for bread and ale in 1521 'at the comyng of Sabrichesworth folke to fet ther may', and made several more payments to the Sawbridgeworth May and the Hatfield May.

Taken together, these entries suggest a parish tradition of a May game involving St. George, and they link eastern Hertfordshire not with the Robin Hood games of the western half of the county, but with East Anglian St. George plays like those at Norwich.[21] In fact, the most elaborate example of a St. George play was the one put on in 1511 at Bassingbourn in Cambridgeshire with the assistance of several other parishes, the Hertfordshire parishes of Royston and Therfield among them.[22] The Stortford records may tell of a similar dramatic collaboration across county boundaries, for while Braughing and Sawbridgeworth are clearly in Hertfordshire, the Hatfield and Stansted mentioned in the accounts may be in Essex. The Hertfordshire boroughs of Hatfield and Stansted Abbots are much further from Bishop's Stortford --

itself right at the Essex -- border than are the Essex villages of Hatfield Heath, Hatfield Broad Oak, and Stansted Mountfitchet.

The difference between the dramatic traditions of eastern and western Hertfordshire surprises at first, since no major topographical barrier separates the two sides of the counties. In fact, the River Lea runs across the county from west to east, passing near Redbourn and flowing through Hatfield, Hertford, and Ware before turning south to join the Thames. Still, it is true that the Lea system primarily drains the eastern half of the county, the Colne system the western half. Moreover, the Lea at one time formed the southwestern border of the Danelaw, a fact perhaps reflected in the Domesday survey, which found the area northeast of the Lea much more heavily populated and cultivated than the area southwest of that river.[23] In population density and in soil content, eastern Hertfordshire had more in common with Essex and Cambridgeshire than with the western half of the county. Whatever its origin, the ancient division persists to this day, as the county has two local history societies, the East Hertfordshire Archaeological Society and the St. Albans and Hertfordshire Architectural and Archaeological Society, the latter concentrating on the western half of the county.

Topographically, Hertfordshire occupies the northern end of the London Basin; it is actually part of the Thames watershed, if not of the Thames Valley. Bedfordshire, on the other hand, is separated from the Thames watershed by the Chiltern Hills, which run along the Hertfordshire-Bedfordshire border. It is drained, instead, by the Great Ouse, which flows easterly across Bedfordshire, through Huntingdonshire and eventually into the Wash beyond King's Lynn. The extant records do not tell us much about what kind of plays Bedfordshire parishes put on, but they do attest to long-standing parish traditions.

The only evidence from churchwardens' accounts comes from Shillington, near the Hertfordshire border and only a few miles from Hexton, with its Robin Hood plays. The accounts for 1575 include receipts for the 'may monye' and payments for a minstrel, for the 'maye mens' dinner and to the 'shot' of Barton. The 'play' of Pulloxhill referred to in a Chancery case of around 1500 may well have been similar in nature, as Pulloxhill is just a few miles west of Shillington. In this case, one John Russell of Pulloxhill was accused of absconding with the four pounds he received from the audience when he and several others 'toke vpon them to make a play' to fund church repairs.[25]

A similar but much earlier case found in a Blunham manor court roll of 1418 reveals just enough to be tantalizing about dramatic activity further north in the county. Richard Naseby accused John Potter of refusing to pay the five shillings he owed Naseby for the rent of 'vestimentes iocalibus' in order to perform a play on Sunday, 5 June 1418.[26] A century later, John Slade of Blunham bequeathed to the church of Barford 'all my play bookes and garmentes with all the properties and other thynges belongyng to the same'.[27] Whether or not these two records involve the same set of costumes cannot be proved; this may have been the John Slade whose father Henry lived in Little Barford, so that he may merely have been returning play books and costumes to Barford that had originated there. Nevertheless, these records do show that plays involving costumes and, by 1528, written texts had a long history in the Blunham area. They also suggest a tradition of private, rather than parish, ownership of this players' gear, a tradition apparently ended by Slade's bequest.

These dramatic records from northern Bedfordshire do not much resemble those from Hertfordshire, but I would be stretching their interpretation too far to find in them a distinctly different dramatic tradition from Hertfordshire's, or to suggest that they connect Bedfordshire with the dramatic traditions found further down the Ouse, in Norfolk and Lincolnshire.

This brief survey of the dramatic traditions of four counties yields no sweeping generalizations about the importance of topography in the spread or development of parish drama. Some of the similarities and differences noticed here may have less to do with location than with the size and structure of the communities that supported the traditions. Both Tewkesbury and Bishop's Stortford appear to have been the center of regional dramatic traditions that involved renting playing paraphernalia from those parishes. Both were ancient market towns with their own officers and burgesses, though powerful lords of the manor dominated local affairs, and a single large parish. Larger towns and cities may have supported travelling players and other forms of entertainment, but those for which we have parish records -- including Gloucester, Winchester, and St. Albans -- yield no evidence of dramatic activity at the parish level. Smaller towns and villages tend to yield records of king ales and May games, whether we look at Andover or Bramley in Hampshire, Redbourn or Braughing in Hertfordshire, or Shillington and Barton in Bedfordshire. Yet one makes these generalizations, too, by leaving out much of the evidence. Even a survey limited to four counties finds the continuities and variations in English parish drama many and complex; we are only beginning to understand them.

Notes

1   Gloucestershire Record Office: P 329 CW 2/1, p. 21, *passim*. In 1579–80, Roger Wiette hired the gear; an entry regarding seat money later in the account identifies him as a resident of the parish (p. 66). Transcriptions of the records of Tewkesbury can be found in Audrey Douglas and Peter H. Greenfield [eds.], *Records of Early English Drama: Cumberland, Westmorland, Gloucestershire*, Toronto, University of Toronto Press, 1986, pp. 335-42.
2   GRO: P 329 CW 2/1, p. 51.
3   Tewkesbury Borough Minute Book. GRO: TBR A 1/1, fol. 24.
4   GRO: P 329 CW 2/1, pp. 130-31. On 'property players', see John C. Coldewey, "That Enterprising Property Player: Semi-Professional Drama in Sixteenth-Century England", *Theatre Notebook*, 31 (1977), p. 6.
5   While 'within the abbey' could mean anywhere within the abbey grounds, rather than specifically within the church, the latter meaning is perhaps more likely, since at the dissolution the monastic buildings were demol-

ished with the exception of the church, which the parish purchased from the Crown for the estimated value of the bells and roof leads -- L483.

6   GRO: P 329 CW 2/1, pp. 65 and 88.

7   Sally-Beth MacLean, "Festive Liturgy and the Dramatic Connection: A Study of Thames Valley Parishes" [unpubl. paper]. See also Alexandra F. Johnston, "What Revels are in Hand?' Dramatic Activities Sponsored by the Parishes", in this collection, pp. 95-104.

8   MacLean, "Festive Liturgy". Also Sandra Billington, *Mock Kings in Medieval Society and Renaissance Drama*, Oxford, Clarendon Press, 1991, pp. 56-57.

9   Hampshire Record Office: 37M85/13/PA/2, fol. 5v. The transcriptions of records of Hampshire, Hertfordshire and Bedfordshire parishes have been prepared in conjunction with my forthcoming edition of the dramatic records of those counties in the Records of Early English Drama series.

10   Hampshire Record Office: 63M70/PW1, pp. 15, 16, 18, and 20.

11   From the churchwardens' accounts of 1563–64. Hampshire Record Office: M63M70/PW1, p. 75.

12   Hampshire Record Office: 75M72/PW1, pp. 47-48.

13   John Foster Williams, *Hampshire Churchwardens' Accounts*, Winchester, 1913. I have not yet seen the original manuscript, which is held at the Surrey Record Office in Guildford.

14   Williams, *Hampshire Churchwardens' Accounts*. The original manuscript is in the library of Corpus Christi College, Oxford.

15   Deposition Book of the Consistory Court of Winchester Diocese. Hampshire Record Office: 21M65/C3/8, p. 128.

16   Public Record Office: STAC 8/262/11.

17   Hampshire Record Office: 70M76A/PW1, fol. 4r-v.

18   British Library Ms. Lansdowne 61, #25, fol. 74.

19   British Library Ms. Add. 6223, fol. 13.

20   Hertfordshire Record Office: D/P 21 5/1, *passim*.

21   Billington, *Mock Kings*, p. 56.

22   Doris Jones-Baker, *The Folklore of Hertfordshire*, London, Batsford, 1977, p. 58.

23   Tony Rook, *A History of Hertfordshire*, Chichester, Phillimore, 1984, pp. 13-18, 30-31, and 35.

24   Bedfordshire Record Office: P44/5/1, fols. 7r-v and 8v.

25   Public Record Office: C. 1/146, no. 48.

26   Bedfordshire Record Office: L26/51, mb. 12d.

27   Archdeacon of Bedford Probate Register. Bedfordshire Record Office: ABP/R 2, fol. 193.

Parish Drama in Worcester
and the Journal of Prior William More

David N. Klausner

The principal source for our knowledge of parish drama in the later Middle Ages and Renaissance has always been, and remains, the parish churchwardens' accounts. Since these accounts usually present a single entry under the heading of receipts or disbursements (occasionally both), they give us relatively clear information on the gross income or expenditure for the play. On occasion, if we are lucky, they even give some indication of the content of the play. What they do not usually indicate is the nature of the receipts -- whether they in some way represent a 'gate', or rather some form of fund-raising -- or a more specific break-down of the expenditures, such as we find in the guild accounts dealing with civic plays. Some further information on the funding of parish plays is given in the weekly account book kept by William More, prior of Worcester, for the years 1517–35.[1] Since the volume surveys a wide area in which the prior held land, owned manors, or had family connections, it provides an extensive view of parish entertainments in the wealthy monastery's sphere of influence.

William More was born William Peers (or Peres) in 1472 in the Shropshire village of 'the More'[2], and entered the priory at Worcester at the age of sixteen. By 1504 he had become kitchener, and within three years sub-prior. He was elected prior on 2 October 1518, and he remained in office until 1535 when he resigned on the condition that he be given a room in the monastery supplied with fuel, and be released from a debt of one hundred pounds. He seems to have survived until after 1558, and to have been buried in the church of Crowle, Worcester, where one of the prior's manors stood, though a local Worcestershire tradition claims that he was stripped of his pension, returned to his family, and died in penury in 1552.[3]

The nature of the entries in More's journal which pertain to parish drama is often closely bound up with the accounting scheme, so a brief consideration of the Prior's accounting methods will be necessary. The account book, or journal, is kept in considerable detail on a weekly basis; each weekly entry seems to divide naturally into three more or less distinct sections. The first line of each entry gives the dating of the week, followed on the next line by the first and most clearly distinct section, a sum for household expenses. These expenses are not itemized, and are not included in the final summation at the end of the weekly entry (implying, I think, that they represent similar or identical recurrent expenses). The only individual payments which occur in this first section are regular alternating payments for 'seyny money' and to the Prior's household players.[4] The normal form of these entries is:

> Ebdomada prima post Natiuitatem sancti Iohannis Baptiste In primis
> for expenses on howsolde -- xx s. ij d.[5]

The second section which follows usually consists of a series of entries representing gifts, grants, rewards, and gratuities. The recipients are often, though not always, named or otherwise identified, and this section of the entry includes frequent payments to professional players, minstrels, bearwards, tumblers, jugglers, and other entertainers. These entries vary considerably, of course, but some representative examples are:

> Item in rewardes to my syster law of bristow when sho was here -- xx s.
> Item in rewardes to dyuers other persons -- xij d. iiij d. viij d. iij d.
> Item rewarded to A Iogellar of the kynges -- xvj d.
> Item rewarded to A seruant of mr swynarton that browȝth A hynde calf -- xij d.
> ...

Item to Iohn englisshe & his iij felowes the kynges pleyeres -- vj.'s viij d.[6]

In the second line the series of sums represents four 'rewards' given to unspecified persons.

The third section of the weekly accounting records what I would call "extraordinary" expenses of a wide variety, including repairs to the prior's manors at Battenhall, Grimley, and Crowle and work on their fish-ponds, as well as major purchases of wine and spices. Here also occur payments made as donations to what are clearly non-professional entertainments; to village singers and dancers and to various Worcester parishes for the performances of plays. I should emphasize that no break is made between these three sections in the manuscript. The first section is always quite distinct because its form is very much the same each week with only minor variations (including, of course, the sum). The boundary between the second and third sections is sometimes less clear.

It is primarily in the third of these sections that references to parish drama and parish entertainments occur. Some of these, like the singers and dancers noted above, involve a parish group brought to the priory or to one of the prior's manors, usually to celebrate a specific occasion such as the priory's dedication day. Some entries, however, refer specifically to parish plays, and it is these which concern us primarily here.

It is frequently difficult to establish the precise auspices of the entertainments cited in these entries; within the city of Worcester, More generally notes the parish, while outside the city the parish, of course, was the village, with no effective administrative distinction between them. Support for the performance of plays by the city parishes is substantiated by an account roll of one of the Worcester obedientiaries a generation before More's time.[7] Nicholas Hanbury, cellarer, some time in the 1470s gave a series of donations to the players of six of the seven Worcester city parishes, omitting only the parish of St. Clement's, most of which lies on the far side of the river from the city.

> ... Et datis lusoribus Ecclesiarum omnium sanctorum sancte Elene sancti Swithini [&] sancti Albani sancti Petri & sancti Michaelis in Wigornia videlicet cuilibet Ecclesie xij d. vj s.[8]

Given the cellarer's position, it is difficult to read this entry as anything other than an official donation by the priory. It thus establishes the possibility of a tradition of priory support for parish plays, but should not be equated with Prior More's donations, which are private rather than official.

The donations made by Prior More to groups identified either by a city parish name or a village name vary considerably, and are worth commenting on individually. In the following commentary the entries are numbered in chronological order and the parish identified. Where it is relevant I also include additional information on the situation of the parish, its connection with Prior More, the state of its own early records, and, in some cases, comments on the amount of the donation.

1. fol. 34r. (12 June 1519, Whitsun)[9]

> Item in rewardes to the pleyeres of seynt mychelles ij s. Item to the seyd churche of seynt myhel v s. iiij d.

The old church of St. Michael physically adjoined the Cathedral at the northwest corner until its demolition in 1840, and the parish included the Cathedral precincts. No churchwardens' accounts or other records survive from this date.

There is no indication that the second payment is related directly to the players (in fact it is likely that it is not), but since it follows immediately in the account and was thus made at least in the same week, it may represent a donation relating to the same occasion or feast.

2. fol. 34v. (19 June 1519)

> Item in rewardes to Robyn whod & hys men for getheryng to
> tewkesbury bruge iij s. iiij d.

The provenance of these players is not mentioned, so it is unclear whether or not they are local, or whether they are amateur or
professional. For a Robin Hood play one might expect amateur
players, but the amount of the payment would suggest that they
are professional, even accounting for Prior More's usual generosity. I include this reference since it is the only Robin Hood entry
not connected directly with a village or parish.

3. fol. 36r. (11 September 1519)

> to Martley pleyeres iiij d.

The village of Martley is located about eight miles northwest
of Worcester. Here, as with most of the village references, the precise relationship of the players to the parish administration (that is,
the churchwardens) cannot be distinguished, since no churchwardens' accounts survive from this date. The amount of the payment
confirms the players' amateur status.

4. fol. 40r. (19 February 1519/20)

> Item rewarded to iiij pleyeres of Evesham iij s. iiij d. / xij d.

The amount of this payment would suggest that these may be
professional players; half a mark is very common payment in the
Prior's journal to a small group of entertainers.[10] The payment of
12d after the slash may not refer to the players at all; miscellane-
ous payments seem frequently to be inserted in this manner without explanation. This performance may have been connected with
Shrove Tuesday, which fell on 20 February.

5. fol. 42v. (17 June 1520)

> Item to pleyers of seynt peturs iiij d. ij d. viij d. vj d. iiij d. iiij d. x
> d. xij d. William taylor

St. Peter's is a suburban parish lying along the London road to the east of the city, on the way to the Prior's manor at Battenhall. The parish has no surviving early records, so it is not possible to ascertain if William Taylor was a churchwarden. As in the previous example, perhaps only the first sum refers to the players.

6. fol. 47r. (30 December 1520)

> Item rewarded to iiij pleyeres of glowceter A pon sonday when the
> balyffs & the xxiiij' dyned with me in the grete hall iij s. iiij d.

This entry clearly refers to professional players, hired as entertainment for a feast. It is included because the amount paid clarifies some of the more ambiguous references, such as the Evesham payment above.

7. fol. 47v. (13 January 1520/21)

> Item rewardes iiij d. ij d. iiij d. xij d. to pleyeres of seynt kenelmes
> [vj] xij d. / ij d.

The chapel of St. Kenelm is located in the northern part of the county, a few miles south of Halesowen. It was a major pilgrimage site in the Middle Ages. No other connection with the Prior is known, and no early records survive.

8. fol. 65r. (10 May 1521, Rogation)

> Item rewardes to the showe of seynt petures xij d. / iiij d. iiij d. xx d.
> iiij d.

The exact meaning of 'show' in this context is not clear, but it would seem to be, 'an extraordinary pageant, procession, or spectacle' (*Oxford English Dictionary*). See further references to parish shows below, and a fuller discussion of their meaning under the last "show" entry (22). As before, the sums indicated after the slash may be unconnected with the donation to St. Peter's.

9. fol. 82r. (4 June 1525, Whitsun)

Item rewardes to vij dawnceres of claynes on trinite sonday xx d.

The large suburban parish of Claines lay about a mile outside the Foregate of the city, along the Droitwich road. The Priory owned considerable property within the bounds of the parish, and the prior had a close connection with it. Payments to the Claines dancers continue over a number of years. Although references to Morris dancing are far less frequent in Worcestershire than in neighbouring Herefordshire, the word 'dance' in both counties seems generally to indicate Morris dancing and may therefore be connected with mumming and other mimetic entertainments.[11]

10. fol. 115v. (16 May 1529, Whitsun)

Item rewardes to certen yong men of seynt Elyns at pleyd Robyn Whod xij d.

The city parish of St. Helen's lies immediately to the west of the Cathedral; churchwardens' accounts survive for the years 1519–20, but contain no references to players.[12] The rather more expansive entry than usual ('certen yong men') might suggest that this donation does not represent a regular occurrence.

11. fol. 119v. (16 January 1529/30)

Item to iiij pleyeres of wurceter on seynt Wlstans day ij s. viij d.

These are most likely professional players; the designation 'of worceter' suggests that they are not performing under parish auspices, but are being hired to celebrate the feast of the Worcester saint. They might, of course, have performed a play dealing with the life of St. Wulstan, but there is no indication that they did so.

12. fol. 121ᵃv. (22 May 1530, Rogation)

> Item to pleyeres at the more on the Assencion day to the vce of A
> church ij s. iiij d.

The More is the Shropshire village of Prior More's birth; this may very well explain the somewhat larger donation than usual. The final phrase 'to the vce of A church' would seem to indicate that the donation is intended for the church's fund-raising rather than for the support of the players.

13. fol. 121ᵃv. (29 May 1530)

> the churche Ale at grymley & a pley. [in left margin]
> Item to the churche Ale at grymley vij s. vj d.

This payment is of considerable interest, for it establishes a clear connection between a church ale and the performance of a play. Grimley was one of the Prior's manors, and again this would explain the extraordinarily generous donation. The journal contains several other donations to church ales, including those at Grimley during the weeks of 10 July 1518, 9 April 1531, and 13 April 1533, though none of these entries is specifically connected with a dramatic performance.

14. fol. 121ᵃv. (12 June 1530, Trinity Sunday)

> Item gyff to the dawnceres of claynes xx d. / to the box of Robyn
> hood &c xij d.

The Robin Hood players in this case appear to be amateurs from the sum they are paid, though it is not clear whether or not they have any connection with the village of Claines.

15. fol. 128r. (7 May 1531)

> In rewardes to the boxe at the showe of seynt petures xij d. / to other
> boxes xvj d. xij d. xij d. iij s. iiijd.

St. Peter's seems to have been an especially active parish; it may also be its proximity of the Prior's manor of Battenhall that aroused his interest and generosity. 'Boxe' appears to be used here in the sense of "donation box"; whether the 'other boxes' are connected in any way with St. Peter's is not entirely clear, but this seems unlikely.[13]

16. fol. 128r. (14 May 1531, Rogation)

> Item to the daunceres of seynt sewthans xij d.

St. Swithin's, a central city parish, is the only city parish to have provided the prior with dancers, with the exception of the unnamed parish in the next entry. Again, no early records or churchwardens' accounts survive for the parish.

17. fol. 128v. (28 May 1531, Whitsun)

> Item to the singeres of the towne on our dedicacion day in the
> morenyng xvj d.
> Item to mynstrelles on our dedicacion day xij d. / to dawnceres of the
> parasshe xx d.

The 'singeres of the towne' would seem to have no distinct parish connection; conversely the parish of the dancers is not mentioned. The week's entry is headed 'Whitsonday at Worceter & batnall'; since 'the parish' would be an unlikely way of referring to Worcester, it seems likely that the reference is to Battenhall, a village about a mile east of the city, and the site of the Prior's principal manor.

18. fol. 129v. (23 July 1531)

> In rewardes to the tenantes of clyve. pleying with Robyn Whot
> Mayde Marion & other vj s. viij d.

The manor of Cleeve Prior northeast of Evesham belonged to the Priory. The prior's tenants are entertaining him; they would certainly not be professional despite the large sum paid them. It is very likely that this entry represents something other than our usual definition of "parish drama" in which the performance is held as a means of fund-raising for the expenses of the parish, that is those items which occur regularly in the churchwardens' disbursements -- repair to the fabric of the church, glazing, baldricks for the bells, etc. Here the rewards seem to be given directly to the individuals. It is, of course, possible that there is really no substantive difference between this entry and those that refer to the players of a particular parish except that the scribe is indicating that they are, in this case, also the prior's tenants.

19. fol. 143v. (6 July 1533)

> the pley at hynwyckes hull [in left margin]
> In rewardes [at] to alhaland churche at the pley holden at hynwyckes
> hull seynt thomas yeven being sonday. & on seynt thomas day beyng
> monday. Whiche pley was kept to the profett of alhaland churche
> vj s. viij d.

Henwick Hall lay to the west of the city of Worcester, across the river. Here the relationship between the play and the parish is clear: the performance, although it is being held in the manor house, is for the benefit of the parish of All Hallows. This entry, unlike the previous one, unequivocally concerns the performance of a play for the purpose of making a profit for the parish.

128

20. fol. 150r. (3 May 1534)

> Item rewardes xiiij d. to pleyeres xvj d. / v s. iiij d. / xvj d. ij s. / to
> the sheowe of seynt Elynes xij d./

Like the references above (8, 15) to the 'showe' of St. Peter's,
this may be a parish performance of some kind under the auspices
of St. Helen's. There is no evidence to indicate that the players in
the previous entry are connected with St. Helen's, except that it is
common in the journal to find related entries closely following
each other.

21. fol. 150v. (17 May 1534)

> Item rewardes to sheowe of seynt Sewthans xx d.

The St. Swithin's show has the same difficulties of interpretation as the other 'shows' (see next entry).

22. fol. 150v. (24 May 1534, Whitsun)

> Item to the box of seynt Andros sheowe on er dedicacion day xij d.
> [&]
> Item in rewardes xij d. xij d. xvj d. ij s.
> Item to seynt Elyns churche Ale xij d.

St. Andrew's, another central city parish, lies along the river to
the west of St. Helen's. No early records or churchwardens' accounts survive. The St. Helen's payment is probably a donation
not necessarily connected with performance or entertainment,
though the payment for the church ale seems to make it clear that
the show (in entry 20) and the church ale are not the same.

The word 'show', which has appeared regularly in the prior's
accounts, is ambiguous in this context and these references may
very well not be to actual dramatic performances, but to a dumb
show or *tableau vivant*, or to a procession. All the references to

shows occur in May, but since there are three weeks between the payments to St. Helen's (3 May) and St. Andrew's (24 May) in 1534, it is not likely that the shows are associated with a specific feast in the Church calendar, though all the 'show' payments fall in the period leading up to Whitsun. The first St. Peter's payment occurs during Rogation Week, the second the week before; in the 1534 payments, Rogation Week falls between the first two payments.

Shows were frequently associated with fairs, as was Chester's elaborate Midsummer Show, which regularly included such entertainments as morris dancing, exotic animals, a giant, and characters from plays.[14] It is probable that these parish shows provided entertainment of a similar kind, though obviously on a much more modest scale.

23. fol. 151r. (31 May 1534, Trinity Sunday)

In rewardes to the dawnceres of claynes xx d.

24. fol. 157r. (9 May 1535)

In rewardes to Edward porter iij s. iiij d. / to the pleyeres of seynt petures xij d.

This is a much clearer record than the payments to St. Peter's 'show' above. Here we are unequivocally dealing with players under parish auspices. The amount is the prior's normal donation to an amateur group.

25. fol. 157v. (30 May 1535)

<R>obyn Whod & litle Iohn of Ombursley xij d.

The village of Ombersley lies about seven miles north of Worcester along the Kidderminster road. Here again the players' amateur status is implied by the amount of the payment. The reference to the village appears simply to indicate their provenance, not that they are performing under parish auspices or to the benefit of the parish.

These rather varied entries provide us with some very useful information. First, from a negative point of view, Prior More's accounts give no evidence at all for the performance of plays of a specifically religious character under parish auspices. Of course, very few of the entries which refer to a parish indicate the nature of the performance, but those which do all refer to Robin Hood plays. The references to singers and dancers associated with a parish (I have not included several payments to 'singers of the town' whose connection to a parish is moot) would suggest further that amateur entertainments under parish auspices were frequently secular. The references to parish 'shows' remain inconclusive, though we have so far no reason to assume that they necessarily imply a religious pageant rather than a secular one. Records from other counties show, on the other hand, that parish performances of a religious nature were common elsewhere.

The timing of the prior's payments is of particular interest. Of the twenty-five entries, seventeen occur in May and June, during the period from a week before Rogation to (at the latest) two weeks after Trinity Sunday, and thus are likely to be connected with the festivities leading up to Whitsun and to Corpus Christi, eleven days later. Many of the entries paid at other times in the year we can see as anomalous in the context of such a large group of payments: the celebration of St. Wulstan's day, the clearly unusual play at Henwick Hall in 1533, the professional players from out-of-town (Evesham in 1519/20, Gloucester in 1520), and the players from outlying locations like Martley, St. Kenelm's, and Ombersley.

The information contained in More's journal casts some further light on parish drama in the early sixteenth century. First, with reference to E. K. Chambers' implied taxonomy in discussing parish drama as a sub-heading of religious drama, the only evidence for the religious character of these plays is their apparent relationship to the feasts of Whitsun and Corpus Christi.[15] The plays themselves may well have been secular, and intended not as a celebration of the church's patron saint or of a sacred festival, but as an economically effective device for raising money for the parish, to cover the never-ending costs of repairs to the fabric of the church and related expenses. Second, it is clear that a frequent choice as a popular and thus effective money-making vehicle was the almost ubiquitous Robin Hood play. It is the only dramatic type referred to specifically in Prior More's journal, and at least two payments connect such performances directly with villages or parishes.

Most usefully, Prior More's journal provides a window on the parish plays of early sixteenth-century Worcestershire which is different from the churchwardens' accounts, giving the perspective of the patron. During the early 1530s, More was accused of extravagance, but his payments to players show little of that.[16] By far his most common donation, either to players or to a 'show' is twelve pence; generous, but hardly extravagant. His payments to professional players is half a mark; this is very much in line with his payments to more obviously professional minstrels and musicians who, especially if they belong to a noble or royal patron, often receive a mark or more. The major recipients of the prior's rewards were the city parishes, outside the city many of the recipients had some direct connection with him -- the village of his birth, for example, receives a relatively lavish donation of 2s 4d. What is most striking about these entries, covering as they do a period of sixteen years, is their lack of regularity. This irregularity can be seen in two ways. First, the Prior's payments to parishes for all forms of entertainment are not consistent over the seventeen years in which they occur, as this chart will show:

Number of annual donations to parish entertainments[17]

1519	2	1525	1	1531	4
1520	2	1526	0	1532	0
1521	1	1527	0	1533	1
1522	0	1528	0	1534	4
1523	0	1529	2	1535	2
1524	0	1530	4		

Most striking is the long gap of seven years from 1522 to 1528 during which only one donation is recorded (to the dancers from the suburban parish of Claines, rather than to a play). This irregularity can be seen in another way as well: other than the local parishes of St. Peter's and St. Helen's, most villages and parishes receive only one donation over this long period. Claines is an exception, since its dancers appear three times in the accounts.

How then do we read this overview of the Prior's donations? Does it indicate that parish plays or 'shows' in Worcestershire were relatively infrequent? The only evidence I can adduce in support of this possibility is that some professional groups, notably the King's Minstrels, appear at the Priory regularly, practically on an annual basis. There is, moreover, ample evidence in the journal of More's generosity. Given these facts, two conclusions seem inescapable. First, it seems very likely that the donations recorded do, in fact, represent a large proportion of the parish plays and shows presented by those parishes with which the prior had a direct relationship. Second, as the lack of repetition in the entries would suggest, the occasions on which such plays and shows were produced appear to have been relatively infrequent, perhaps motivated more by financial need rather than by tradition. Unfortunately, the lack of supporting churchwardens' accounts or other documentation from the parishes themselves make it impossible to substantiate this possibility. It does, however, mean that it would be unwise to treat the relatively large number of references to parish entertainments in More's journal as evidence of an extensive and thriving tradition in Worcestershire, occurring, as they do, over a period of seventeen years.

Notes

1   Worcester Cathedral Library, Ms. A-11, a paper quarto volume, 207x 312mm; i+158+i, foliated 1-121a, 121b-157. The manuscript was edited by E. S. Fegan for the Worcestershire Historical Society (London, 1913–14); extensive excerpts are printed in D. N. Klausner [ed.], *Records of Early English Drama: Herefordshire and Worcestershire*, Toronto, University of Toronto Press, 1990, pp. 459-530.

2   The village regularly appears in early documents as 'la Mora'.

3   *DNB* xiii 897; More gives various details of his life at the beginning of his Journal. The tradition of his earlier death is recorded in a note inserted in the manuscript of the journal by Canon J. Willis Bund, citing the following entry in the Alverton, Warwick, parish register:

Anno Domini 1552   William more was sometyme Prior of Worceter was buried the xvjth of September.

4   The Prior's household players, the 'seyny' money payments, and the relationship between them are discussed fully in Klausner, *REED: Herefordshire and Worcestershire*, pp. 307-08, and Appendix III, pp. 541-47.

5   1519; fol. 34v. These household expense entries continue almost identically (with varying sums) for the eighteen years of the journal. In the quotations from Prior More's journal which follow, abbreviations have been silently expanded and interlinear additions have been dropped to the line. With the exception of the examples given on this page, all subsequent quotations may be found in a form which indicates abbreviations and interlinear additions in Klausner, *REED: Herefordshire and Worcestershire*, pp. 462-529.

6   The first group of entries is from 1519, fol. 35r.; the last entry is from 1529, fol. 117v.

7   Hereford Cathedral Library, Roll R707, mb 5. The date has been torn off; Hanbury held the office of cellarer through most of the 1470s.

8   Klausner, *REED: Herefordshire and Worcestershire*, p. 404.

9   All these entries may be found in Klausner, *REED: Herefordshire and Worcestershire*, pp. 462-529.

10 Compare the same amount paid to 'iiij pleyeres of glowceter' (fol. 47r) and to 'iiij pleyeres of coventrie' (fol. 113r).

11 The prosecutions of the consistory courts of both the Hereford and Worcester dioceses make this clear, sometimes referring to 'Morrice' dancing,

and sometimes simply to 'dancing', often within the context of the same prosecution. See, for example, Klausner, *REED: Herefordshire and Worcestershire*, p. 169, l. 31 and p. 171, l. 10.

12 The surviving accounts are included in J. Amphlett [ed.], *The Churchwardens' Accounts of St. Michael's in Bedwardine, Worcester*, Oxford, Worcestershire Historical Society, 1896, pp. 1-8.

13 Donations to 'boxes' without any further specification are also made at Overbury and Cropthorne during the week of 7 April 1521, and at Harvington during the week of 14 April 1521.

14 L. Clopper [ed.], *Records of Early English Drama: Chester*, Toronto: Toronto University Press, 1979, esp. pp. lii-liii.

15 E. K. Chambers, *The Medieval Stage*, Oxford, Oxford University Press, 1903, vol. II, pp. 106-48, esp. pp. 121-22.

16 The details of the case brought by John Musard are summarized in Klausner, *REED: Herefordshire and Worcestershire*, p. 305.

17 For the purpose of this chart the year is begun on 25 March.

'Interludum Passionis Domini':
Parish Drama in Medieval New Romney

James M. Gibson

For at least one hundred and forty years before its last attempted
revival in 1568, the townspeople of New Romney performed their
passion play, the *interludum passionis domini*, at Whitsuntide. A
1516 memorandum in the chamberlains' accounts describes a
meeting of the barons, jurats, and commonalty in the common
place to elect five playwardens, 'for the holding of the play of the
passion of Christ as from ancient time they have been accustomed
to do.'[1] Sixty years earlier, in 1456, the play first appears in the
New Romney records, when John Craye and Thomas a Nasshe,
wardens of the play of the Resurrection, brought an action for debt
and damages against John Lylye; in the records of the nearby
town of Lydd players of New Romney were paid for performing
as early as 1428.[2] How much further back the ancient custom ex-
tends no one knows, for both the playbook and most of the playwardens' accounts have disappeared.

What we do know comes from three principal sources: fragmentary playwardens' accounts, probably dating from 1488 and
now bound with the 1469-92 chamberlains' accounts[3], recognizances sworn by the actors during the 1556 revival[4], and extensive
memoranda in the court book and accounts of the town chamberlain during the 1560 performance.[5] Apart from these sources only
sporadic references to the play appear in the surviving town records, such tantalizing items as the payments 'for serten playeng
gere'[6] and 'expences at the rehersyng of the play in lent'[7] during
1539, a year that saw payments in the chamberlains' accounts to
nine visiting companies of players, but no further expenses for

New Romney's own play. In 1555 and again in 1560 John For-
sett was paid for copying out the parts of the play to be used in re-
hearsal, yet no copy of the playbook survives.[8] Enough information does exist, however, to reconstruct a reasonable picture of the
content and administration of the New Romney passion play.

Many of the *dramatis personae* of the passion play can be
gleaned from the surviving records. Three recognizances sworn
before bailiff Richard Bunting and the jurats of New Romney on
27 December 1555, committing the actors to learn and rehearse
their parts for the performance at Pentecost, form a nearly complete cast list. On the first appear Herod, accompanied by two
knights and a messenger, Pilate and his messenger, Caiaphas and
his messenger, Annas and his handmaid, the second devil, and six
tormentors, 'Mischaunce', 'Falce at Nede', 'Vntrust', 'Faynthart', 'Vnhappe', and 'Evyll Grace'.[9] The second recognizance
lists the blind man, his boy, his mother and father, SS. Peter, Simon, Matthew, Andrew, John, James, James the Lesser, Thomas,
Philip, Bartholomew, and Jude, Judas the traitor, two Pharisees,
Lazarus, Martha, Mary Magdalen, Martha's servant, a neighbor,
and another Jew.[10] The third adds a doctor, the Virgin Mary, three
princes, Malchus, Mary Salome, the Third Devil, and Simon of
Cyrene.[11] Other characters emerge from passing references in the
fifteenth-century playwardens' accounts -- 'vj yerdis of blankett
for the bisshopp gownys'[12] -- or in the 1560 chamberlains' accounts: 'shepeskynes for ye godheddes coote'[13], 'a sho set on the
centuryons horsse'[14], and 'the payntyng of St. Iohn Baptistes
coote.'[15] Further payments testify to numerous minstrels, waits,
bann criers, and a fool, but notable absentees include the first and
second soldier, the first and second thief, the angel, Lucifer, and
Christ.[16]

The surviving records also reveal hints about the passion
play's structure and staging. The accounts refer to four separate
plays within the passion play, and other memoranda and payments
for properties suggest further division of these four plays into

several scenes.[17] A 1560 memorandum, for example, appoints builders for seven stages: 'Pilates & princes stage', 'Annas stage & the Tormentours', 'the Pharisees stage', 'herodes stage', 'heaven', 'the Cave' including 'the iij crosses', and 'hell'.[18] The accounts refer to yet other stages and properties, which, together with the characters mentioned in the recognizances, permit a conjectural reconstruction of the New Romney passion play as a cycle of four plays organized along the following lines.

The first play, a sequence of five scenes mostly unique to the Gospel of John, covered the ministry of Christ focusing on his confrontation with the Pharisees: the baptism of Jesus and choosing of the disciples (John 1), the woman of Samaria (John 4), the healing of the blind man (John 9), the raising of Lazarus (John 11), and the triumphal entry (John 12). The sequence opened with John the Baptist baptising Jesus -- witness the payments in the accounts for painting John the Baptist's coat.[19] The recognizances that include the twelve disciples and two Pharisees and the memorandum that mentions the Pharisees stage both point toward the version of Jesus' baptism narrated in John 1, where John debates with the Pharisees before baptising Jesus and then sends to Jesus two of his own disciples, who subsequently recruit the rest.[20] The second scene in the sequence, a unique appearance in the cycle plays of the Samaritan woman at the well, may be deduced from the payment in 1560 to Richard Hawkins 'for a dayes worcke to set vp the cytye of samary'[21], an allusion to the Vulgate's *civitatem Samariae* in John 4:5. This story, in which Jesus offers water and forgiveness to the Samaritan woman, no doubt also included parts for the disciples and the two Pharisees. Cast lists for the next two scenes, the healing of the blind man and the raising of Lazarus, appear in the 1555 recognizances.[22] Again each story in the Gospel of John features a confrontation with the Pharisees, who plot the death of Lazarus and the death of Jesus just before the triumphal entry narrated in John 12, and both scenes were probably played on the Pharisees stage. The entry of Jesus into Jerusalem, deduced from the payment in the fifteenth-century playwardens' fragment for 'ij halters for the asse'[23], concludes the ministry sequence at a triumphal moment for Jesus, as the Pharisees exclaim to themselves in John 12:18, 'Perceive how you prevail nothing? behold, the world is gone after him.' Structurally, then, the first play, or ministry sequence, pits the Pharisees against Jesus in a series of confrontations drawn from the Gospel of John, rising to a climax in the triumphal entry and preparing the way for the reversal of action in the passion sequence of the second play.

Play One: The Ministry of Christ

Baptism of Jesus	The Samaritan Woman	Healing the Blind Man	Raising of Lazarus	Triumphal Entry
[Jesus]	[Jesus]	[Jesus]	[Jesus]	[Jesus]
[John the Baptist]				
Peter	Peter	Peter	Peter	Peter
Simon	Simon	Simon	Simon	Simon
Matthew	Matthew	Matthew	Matthew	Matthew
Andrew	Andrew	Andrew	Andrew	Andrew
John	John	John	John	John
James	James	James	James	James
James the Lesser	James the Lesser	James the Lesser	James the Lesser	James the Lesser
Thomas	Thomas	Thomas	Thomas	Thomas
Philip	Philip	Philip	Philip	Philip
Bartholomew	Bartholomew	Bartholomew	Bartholomew	Bartholomew
Jude	Jude	Jude	Jude	Jude
Judas the traitor	Judas the traitor	Judas the traitor	Judas the traitor	Judas the traitor
First Pharisee		First Pharisee	First Pharisee	First Pharisee
Second Pharisee		Second Pharisee	Second Pharisee	Second Pharisee
	[First Jew]		Neighbour	Neighbour
	[Second Jew]		Another Jew	Another Jew
	[Woman of Samaria]			
		Blind Man		
		His Boy		
		Mother		
		Father		
		Doctor		
			Lazarus	Lazarus
			[Mary]	[Mary]
			Martha	Martha
			Her Servant	Her servant

140

The second play, the Betrayal and Buffeting, portrays the arrest and trial of Jesus. Payments in the 1560 accounts to Thomas Starre 'for dressing of the pascall lambe'[24] suggest that the play opened with the Last Supper. The remaining scenes, deduced from the recognizances and from the list of stages, follow the traditional sequence of events found in all the gospels, although the inclusion of Malchus in the cast list indicates that the compiler of the play was probably still relying principally on the Gospel of John, as only that evangelist names the servant of the high priest whose ear was cut off and restored during the arrest.[25] The trial scenes take place successively on Annas's stage with Caiaphas, Annas, their servants, and possibly the bishop mentioned in the account fragment; on Pilate's stage with Pilate, his messenger, who also doubled as Caiaphas' messenger, and the three princes; and on Herod's stage with Herod and his two knights, the second of which also doubled as his messenger. Most notable here are the six personified tormentors dressed in elaborate costumes and masks -- 'Mischaunce', 'Falce at Nede', 'Vntrust', 'Faynthart', 'Vnhappe', and 'Evyll Grace' -- who shared the stage with Annas and Caiaphas. As in Thomas Preston's *Cambyses* and other sixteenth-century hybrid plays, these abstract personifications rubbed shoulders with historical characters, depicting in stylized form emotions that later sixteenth-century dramatists learned to show realistically through speech and action. When Jesus appeared before Annas, the tormentors objectified or portrayed outwardly the torment he must have felt inwardly: 'Falce at Nede' -- the denial of Peter, 'Vntrust' -- the betrayal of Judas, Faynthart -- the desertion by the remaining disciples, Evyll Grace -- the mockery of Annas and Caiaphas, 'Vnhappe' -- the pain of scourge and crown of thorns.

Play Two: Betrayal and Buffetting

The Last Supper	Betrayal and Arrest	Christ before Annas	Christ before Pilate	Christ before Herod
[Jesus]	[Jesus]	[Jesus]	[Jesus]	[Jesus]
Peter	Peter	Peter		
Simon	Simon			
Matthew	Matthew			
Andrew	Andrew			
John	John			
James the Lesser	James the Lesser			
Thomas	Thomas			
Philip	Philip			
Bartholomew	Bartholomew			
Jude	Jude			
Judas the traitor	Judas the traitor			
	Malchus	Malchus		
	[First Soldier]	[First Soldier]	[First Soldier]	[First Soldier]
	[Second Soldier]	[Second Soldier]	[Second Soldier]	[Second Soldier]
		Caiaphas		
		His messenger	Messenger	
		Annas		
		His handmaid		
		Mischaunce		
		Falce at Nede		
		Vntrust		
		Faynthart		
		Vnhappe		
		Evyll Grace		
			Pilate	
			First Prince	
			Second Prince	
			Third Prince	
				Herod
				First Knight
				Second Knight
				Messenger

3.   The third play, depicting Christ's death and descent into hell, probably consisted of three scenes, each with its own stage or center of action noted in the 1560 memorandum listing the builders of

142

the stages.[26] Three crosses are specified for the crucifixion scene, and the recognizances include parts for Simon of Cyrene, the three Mary's, and John.[27] No soldiers are listed, but the 1560 accounts include payments for swords and for the shoeing of the centurion's horse.[28] If the playwright were still following the Gospel of John, then Pilate, Annas, Caiaphas, and the two Pharisees would have swelled the group around the cross.[29] A burial scene in 'the cave' featuring Nicodemus and Joseph of Arimathea, who also appear in the Gospel of John, may have followed although neither character appears in the recognizances.[30] The harrowing of hell may be safely inferred both from the hell stage[31] and from the mention of the second and third devils[32], the former doubling as Annas in the second play. Among other stage properties the fifteenth-century account fragment calls for *campanis pro inferno*[33] or Hell's bells, probably Morris bells strapped to the arms and legs of the devils.

Play Three: Death and Descent into Hell

Crucifixion	Burial	Harrowing of Hell
[Jesus]	[Jesus]	[Jesus]
Simon of Cyrene		
Blessed Virgin Mary		
Mary Salome		
Mary Magdalene		
John		
Pilate	Pilate	
Annas		
Caiaphas		
Centurion	Centurion	
[First Soldier]	[First Soldier]	
[Second Soldier]	[Second Soldier]	
[First Thief]		
[Second Thief]		
	[Nicodemus]	
	[Joseph of Arimathea]	
		[Lucifer]
		Second Devil
		Third Devil
		[Patriarchs]

143

4.

The last play, 'ludi de resureccione', is the only play specifically mentioned by name in the New Romney records.[34] The action
here revolved around two centers -- 'the cave' for the resurrection
scene and 'heaven' for the ascension.[35] The former may have featured Mary Magdalene, mentioned in the recognizances, as does
the resurrection account in John 20.[36] The latter scene apparently
featured God the Father, who appeared on the heaven stage dressed in his white 'godheddes coote', a coat made from six sheep-
skins.[37] No expense was spared on this coat or other costumes,
for during the 1520s and 1530s the playwardens solicited the help
of New Romney resident Richard Gibson, Yeoman of the Tents
and Sergeant-at-Arms for Henry VIII, who advised them on ap-
parel for the play.[38]

Play Four: The Resurrection and Ascension

Resurrection	Ascension
[Jesus]	[Jesus]
Blessed Virgin Mary	
Mary Salome	
Mary Magdalene	
Peter	Peter
John	John
[Angel]	[Angel]
	God the Father
	Simon
	Matthew
	Andrew
	John
	James the Lesser
	Thomas
	Philip
	Bartholomew
	Jude

As well as revealing a fully developed Passion play in the
south of England, depicting scenes from Christ's baptism to ascension performed on fixed staging, the New Romney records

144

also provide valuable clues to play administration and finance in a town that lacked an organized guild structure. Performances oc- curred at various times during the summer. In 1560, for example, the accounts mention four successive play days at Whitsun begin- ning on 3 June, Whit Monday.[39] Another performance is recorded the same year on Sunday, 14 July.[40] In 1562, performances lasting several days concluded on 10 August, the feast day of St. Lau- rence and New Romney's fair day.[41] Long before these summer performances, however, the town organized to prepare and re- hearse its play.

First came the election of playwardens, by ancient custom cho- sen by the bailiff, jurats, and commonalty of New Romney gather- ed in the common place. On 14 December 1516, for example, the town elected from among the jurats and commoners five men -- Richard Stuppeny, Christopher Hensfeld, Robert Paris, John Bun- ting, and William Bedell -- to serve as playwardens.[42] In April 1560 jurats Robert Kennet and Thomas Ederyck and commoners John Parker and Richard Godfreye were elected.[43]

Then came the casting of the play and the distribution of parts. For the performance of the play at Whitsuntide 1556, the players, an all-male cast, were chosen and the parts distributed on 27 De- cember 1555.[44] Recognizances were sworn before bailiff John Bunting, committing the players to learn their parts by Pentecost, barring an act of God or intervention of the King or Queen. Be- fore that date the town clerk had copied each man's part from the playbook ready for distribution. The playbook itself remained in the custody of the town clerk and appears in several inventories of the town records. Whenever it was needed for rehearsing of the play, careful records were made of its borrowing and return.[45]

For townspeople not chosen as players, many jobs remained to be done. In the 1560 revival, for example, a general meeting of all the inhabitants of New Romney was held in St. Nicholas church on 18 February at which it was recorded what each person agreed to contribute to the play: most offered two or three days' labor.

Mr. Holton agreed to build heaven, Richard Godfrey offered to build his portion of the stage. Thomas Ederycke volunteered 'four lodes with his wayne & fours dayes worck', and Mr. Cheseman paid twenty shillings so that he 'be not charged with any thinge or any offyce touchinge the playe.'[46] On 13 May, apparently distant enough from that February meeting for some people to have forgotten what they had promised, it was decreed in a general meeting of the bailiff, jurats, and commonalty, 'that every man that is here appoynted to buylde the stages neglectynge & not doynge his duytie in buyldynge the same at such tyme as shalbe appoynted by mr Baylif & Iurates shall lose forfeyt and paye to thuse of the towne xx s. to be furthe wyth levyed by mr Baylyves serieaunt.'[47] Production of the play that year, including directing rehearsals and fetching supplies from London, was arranged by the 'devysor' Gover Martin.[48]

To advertise the play, bann criers dressed in costume travelled to the surrounding villages and towns of Romney Marsh, providing a foretaste of the entertainment to come -- witness the payment of ten shillings in 1560 for 'iiij beardes & heares for the bane cryers & a heare and beard for the ffoole.'[49] They gathered money towards the play expenses -- in the playwardens' account fragment three shillings and four pence each from Ivychurch and Brookland, five shillings from Folkestone, and six shillings and eight pence each from Hythe and Lydd.[50] Often they were bread and beer -- at Lydd, for example, the New Romney bann criers were entertained in 1479, 1516, 1525, 1532, 1539, and 1560.[51]

Although the bann criers did collect some money in advance of the performance, the majority of expenses for rehearsals, costumes, and properties was met by loans to be paid back from the play's receipts. In 1503, for example, the playwardens received a loan directly from the town chamberlain[52]; in 1497 and again in 1505 the chamberlain reimbursed various townspeople who had themselves loaned money to the playwardens.[53] In 1560 gifts toward expenses were received from nearby Lydd and Ivychurch.[54]

At the performance itself money gatherers collected money from the audience. The fifteenth-century playwardens' fragment shows receipts from five money gathers at the second play, and in 1560 receipts are totaled for each play day.[55]

Financed by the town chamberlain, advertised by bann criers, administered by playwardens, and performed by parishioners, the New Romney passion play, in contrast to the northern cycle plays, offers a different model for the production of medieval biblical drama. Although New Romney lacks the extensive guild records of York or the multiple copies of the Chester playbook, the surviving records nevertheless do offer a fascinating view of the *interludum passionis domini*, New Romney's contribution to medieval parish drama.

Notes

1   Maidstone, Centre for Kentish Studies, NR/FAc6, fol. 71v.
2   *ibid.*, NR/JB2, fol. 23v; Lydd, Borough Records, LY/FAcl. fol. 4v.
3   Maidstone, Centre for Kentish Studies, NR/FAc4, fols. 310v-312r.
4   *ibid.*, NR/JB6, fols. 215r-216r.
5   *ibid.*, NR/JB7, fols. 40r-41r, 49r, 67v-68r; NR/FAc7, 116v, 118r-125v.
6   *ibid.*, NR/FAc7, fol. 37r.
7   *ibid.*, fol. 38r.
8   *ibid.*, fols. 93v, 118a, 120v.
9   *ibid.*, NR/JB6, fol. 215r.
10 *ibid.*, fol. 215v.
11 *ibid.*, fol. 216r.
12 *ibid.*, NR/FAc4, fol. 311r.
13 *ibid.*, NR/FAc7, fol. 123r.
14 *ibid.*, fol. 119r.
15 *ibid.*, fol. 122r.
16 *ibid.*, fols. 121r, 122v, 124v.
17 *ibid.*, NR/JB7, fol. 116v.
18 *ibid.*, fol. 68r.
19 *ibid.*, NR/FAc7, fol. 122r.
20 *ibid.*, NR/JB6, fol. 215v.; NR/JB7, fol. 68r.
21 *ibid.*, NR/FAc7, fol. 122r.
22 *ibid.*, NR/JB6, fol. 215v.
23 *ibid.*, NR/FAc4, fol. 310v.

24 *ibid.*, NR/FAc7, fol. 124v.
25 *ibid.*, NR/JB6, fol. 215r; *ibid.*, NR/JB7, fol. 68r; John 18:10.
26 *ibid.*, NR/JB7, fol. 68r.
27 *ibid.*, NR/JB6, fols. 215v-216r.
28 *ibid.*, NR/FAc7, fols. 118v, 119r, 122v, 123r.
29 John 19:17-37.
30 John 19:38-42.
31 Maidstone, Centre for Kentish Studies, NR/JB7, fol. 68r.
32 *ibid.*, NR/JB6, fols. 215r, 216r.
33 *ibid.*, NR/FAc4, fol. 310v.
34 *ibid.*, NR/JB2, fol. 23v.
35 *ibid.*, NR/JB7, fol. 68r.
36 *ibid.*, NR/JB6, fol. 215v.
37 *ibid.*, NR/FAc7, fol. 123r.
38 *ibid.*, NR/FAc3, fol. 137r.
39 *ibid.*, NR/FAc7, fol. 116v.
40 *ibid.*, NR/JB7, fol. 67v.
41 *ibid.*, NR/JQpl/4, fol. 1r.
42 *ibid.*, NR/FAc6, fol. 71v.
43 *ibid.*, NR/JB7, fol. 49r.
44 *ibid.*, NR/JB6, fols. 215r-216r.
45 *ibid.*, NR/FAc6, fol. 72r; N/RJB6, fols. 92v-93r; NR/FAc7, fol. 93v.
46 *ibid.*, NR/JB7, fols. 40r-41r.
47 *ibid.*, NR/JB7, fol. 67v.
48 *ibid.*, NR/FAc7, fols. 118r, 119v, 123v.
49 *ibid.*, NR/FAc7, fol. 121r.
50 *ibid.*, NR/FAc4, fol. 311v.
51 Lydd, Borough Records, Ly/FAc1, fols. 160v/161r; LY/FAc2, pp. 29, 110, 175, 226; LY/FAc3, p. 110.
52 Maidstone, Centre for Kentish Studies, NR/FAc5, fol. 118r.
53 *ibid.*, NR/FAc5, fols. 77r, 132v.
54 *ibid.*, NR/FAc7, fol. 116v.
55 *ibid.*, NR/FAc4, fol. 310v; NR/FAc7, fol. 116v.

A Parish Play in the West Riding of Yorkshire

John M. Wasson

The town of Methley, southeast of Leeds and northeast of Wakefield, was a prosperous place in the Middle Ages and Renaissance, the lords of the manor being a branch of the wealthy and important Savile family. St. Oswald, the parish church, was one of the largest and richest in the entire West Riding, the largest county in England. It had a number of wealthy patrons, including Sir Robert Waterton (†1424), who founded the south chapel, Lord Welles (†1461), who is buried there, and Sir John Savile (†1606) and his son Sir Henry (†1632), who owned the Methley Hall mansion and are also buried in the church. The present church building was apparently erected in the thirteenth century and much expanded in the early fourteenth and again late in the fifteenth -- evidence of continuing prosperity.[1] That prosperity seems to have been still in existence in the early seventeenth century, when the Saviles were doubling the size of Methley Hall, and a parish play was presented four days in a row, Monday through Thursday of Whitsun week, 13–16 June 1614, which attracted 'a multitude of people' to see the performances.[2]

Interestingly, and I think uncommonly, the title of the parish play was *Canimore and Lionley*, its performance having been noted by a member of the local gentry, Richard Shann, in his commonplace book, perhaps only because six members of the Shann family were in the production. There is no other extant local reference to the play, and I have been unable to find another single mention of such a play anywhere -- not in the *Short Title Catalogue*, the *Stationers' Register*, or in the records of Oxford and Cambridge Universities, even though Shann's entry suggests that it was a new play.

The only play I have been able to find with anything close to a similar title was one acted at court by the King's Men on 20 May 1613, a year before this Methley performance. Thomas Shelton had published his translation of *Don Quixote* in 1612, and apparently John Fletcher had written a play based on one of the several romances inserted by Cervantes toward the end of Part One. Fletcher's play is not extant, but it was rewritten in 1727 by Lewis Theobald, who claimed to have three manuscript copies of it and who titled his version of it *Double Falsehood, or The Distracted Lovers*. Fletcher's original, titled *Cardenio*, was based on the story of Cardenio and his childhood sweetheart, Luscinda. Cardenio, preparing to marry her, seeks the help of his lascivious and false friend, Fernando, who when he meets her decides he wants her for himself. He dupes Cardenio and forces Luscinda to marry him instead. She intends to refuse but cannot bring herself not to say 'I do', although she then faints at the altar. In the meantime, Cardenio goes insane with grief at her supposed infidelity. When she recovers, Luscinda flees to a nunnery to save her virginity. Cardenio eventually recovers his sanity and, ultimately, the two lovers are reunited.

It might be possible, since the dating is right for a production the next year in Methley, that Cardenio and Luscinda became Canimore and Lionley by the time the script reached Yorkshire. But the cast list which Richard Shann included in his commonplace book makes this possibility seem not likely. For instance, there is no counterpart in that list for the traitor Fernando nor for his fiancée, whom he had betrayed to marry Luscinda. In fact, the only other female role in that list besides Lionley is her maid, Meldine.

Unfortunately, then, we thus have no text for the Methley parish play, nor even a plot summary. We have only Richard Shann's assurance that it was 'a very fyne Historie or Stage play', and his list of who performed which parts. That list, however, tells us quite a bit about what kind of play it was. One normally expects a parish play to be either a folk play -- e.g., on Robin Hood or St. George -- or a religious play either on the patron saint of the church or, like those sometimes still performed today, a nativity play at Christmas or a resurrection play at Easter. But the Methley parish play seems almost certainly to have been a knightly romance. Twenty characters are mentioned in the cast list (to be performed by seventeen actors), but not one of them is a religious figure. Of the title characters, Prince Canimore is the son of a King Padamon and Princess Lionley is the daughter of a King Graniorn. In addition to the usual royal retinue of a duke, earls and knights, the cast includes two knight adventurers, a country man, a vice figure or fool called 'Invention the paracite', a commoner and of course a ghost. Clearly we are not dealing with biblical history here or with any European history of which this author is aware. These are the kinds of characters of which fairy tales and dramatic romances are made, from *Sir Clyomon and Sir Clamydes* of about 1570 to *The Tempest* of 1611. As I have never before come across a parish play which was not either religious or folk, I am curious to know if this Methley play is an anomaly.[3]

The play was acted not in the parish church but in a large barn next to the parsonage -- possibly originally the tithe barn. Clearly from the commonplace book entry, Richard Shann was more interested in recording who was in the play than in the plot or staging. Curiously, we find the same kind of doubling that one expects in the London professional drama of the Renaissance. Richard Dickonsonne, for instance, played both of the kings' parts. Francis Shann played King Graniorn's son, and Robert Shann played his daughter Lionley. Another Shann, Richard, played Lionley's maid. (This was probably not the author of the commonplace book, as he was then in his mid-fifties and would hardly pass as a maid unless it were someone like Juliet's nurse. In any case, if he were personally in the play he would have said so in his commonplace book.) One Thomas Shann acted the part of Duke Gordon, another Thomas played a knight called Sir Brocadon, and a third Thomas Shann, apparently a relative from Hungate, was one of the knight adventurers. A Thomas Burton played Earl Carthagan, while Francis Burton was the hero, Prince Canimore.[4] Thomas Johnson was the other knight adventurer, and Robert Marshall doubled as a knight and the sword-bearer -- doubtless when the scene shifted from one kingdom to the other, whatever those kingdoms were supposed to be. A third Burton, William, doubled as the country man and the ghost. His son, also William, played Invention the parasite. Thomas Scofeild was the Earl of Edios. The writer seems to have forgotten what role Richard Burton performed, as his name is listed but with no part beside it. (One would rather expect someone with the name of Richard Burton to have a major role.) Toby Burton, however, was a page, and finally Gilbert Robert is listed as playing 'one of the Comans part'.

Clearly, as no other commoners are set down in the cast list, there was more doubling than Shann could remember. In any case, although the cast which Shann did recall seems to be dominated by six members of the Shann family and five from the Burton family, there are enough other names to make clear that this was a parish of Methley play, hardly a private family performance. There were at this time a number of Shanns living in the parish of Methley. At the jury of the Great Court at Michaelmas 1616, for example, among the sixteen jurors were Robert Shann Sr, Thomas Shann, Richard Shann, and William Shann. In 1617, seven different Shanns appear in a cessment for copyhold woods. The fact that the play was acted in a big barn near the parsonage, not in a manor house, underlines the conclusion that *Canimore and Lionley* was a parish production.

As I have not come across a cast list like this elsewhere in any of the five counties whose records I have examined, and as none of the published Records of Early English Drama or Malone Society Collections volumes gives any similar lists for parish dramas, I am particularly interested to know if anyone else has come across such a list, especially one with this kind of doubling. One can understand why a professional acting company, with only ten to sixteen players in 1614, would necessarily have to resort to doubling (none of Shakespeare's plays, for example, is written for more than sixteen actors). Why a large parish like Methley, with hundreds of people to select from, should choose to double roles is less clear. Second, as parish folk activities frequently employed women -- Robin Hood's Maid Marian or the Queen of the May or the Summer Queen -- one wonders why *Canimore and Lionley* uses male actors for the only two female roles.[5] Numerous professional acting companies came into the West Riding of Yorkshire -- fifty-one different companies between 1450 and 1632 at preliminary cursory count -- and possibly the person who obtained a copy of the play simply was accustomed to boy actors playing women's roles in professional plays such as this one seems to be and thus did not think of casting women in those two roles.[6] Perhaps the decision was simply a matter of accommodation to now unknown performance factors, but as neither Lionley nor her maid has to double, using boys does seem strange.

We know, however, from extant regulations that schoolmasters normally were expected to have their boys perform a play at least once a year and that many schoolmasters -- John Redford, Nicholas Udall, and the unnamed Doncaster master, among many others -- wrote their own plays for their students. If *Canimore and Lionley* were a school play, such category certainly would explain why the actors all were male. One can hardly think that the reason was the Puritan objection to women as performers (or to their doing anything else in public), since Yorkshire at this time was not exactly a Puritan stronghold. In fact, Richard Shann's son wrote in the commonplace book after his father died in 1627, 'Richard Shanne, ffather of the aboue-written Thomas Shanne died the xvth day of July beinge Sonday at thre of the clocke in the afternoone of A consuming consumption, and was buried vnder the stone of the Lady Queare end the xvj day therof. He dyed A Romaine Catholicke'.[7]

One regrets having no more information about what must have been a very unusual parish drama -- the kind of thing one would like to have a copy of in order to demolish some ninety-year-old assumptions about the nature of parish drama. As the matter stands, given the cast list and nothing else, all one can say is that it must have been a fairly typical knightly romance, of the sort Sir Philip Sidney distrusted because they appealed to common emotions rather than to intellect, and because they jumped from one country to another and skipped over years instead of obeying the classical unities.[8] With the two knights errant in the cast, and a prince from one country and a princess from another, one is reminded of the early *Sir Clyomon and Sir Clamydes*, with knights doing brave deeds not so much for virtue's sake as to win the love of a beautiful woman. Certainly with one actor playing the kings of two countries, the performance had to jump from one country to another, as in *Winter's Tale* or *Cymbeline*. One only hopes that Canimore proved himself worthy of Lionley and that they lived happily ever after.

Whether this 'very fyne Historie or Stage play' was devoid or not of Sidney's demand for intellectual content, the audiences must have enjoyed the show since they crowded the barn for four days in a row. In fact, on Tuesday, 14 June, a tenth of the people who came to see it could not cram into the big barn, Shann reports. There is a reason for the larger crowd on that Tuesday: the parishioners also held a rushbearing at the church that day. It is not easy to describe rushbearings, as they seemed to vary considerably from one parish to another. Suffice it to say that this particular one certainly impressed Richard Shann, although the *Oxford English Dictionary* is unhelpful in explaining exactly what it was that most impressed him. Shann writes that along with the parishioners there was 'a great company of verie fayre Pitopps as we call them, most richlie bewtefied with Slaves and other silkes'. Appealing as those 'verie fayre Pitopps' must have been to the Methley community, their description escapes this writer's efforts.

Shann's final observation about this celebration is a touching one, but it also gives some idea of the importance of rushbearings in the North. He writes, 'vpon whitsonn even being the xjth of June 1614 my doughter Ann was verie sicke by reason of a desinesse that was in her heade, but god be prased she did recover soone after, for she went to the church with the Rush bearinge'. Shann praised God for this miracle; a more cynical suspicion is that no teenage girl, dizzy or not, would have chosen to stay in bed during a rushbearing with all those very fair Pitopps.

Whether the parish of Methley was unique in its choice of dramatic production will have to await further detective work, but it presently seems to be most novel. Without the original play manuscript or a clue about the plotline for Canimore's and Lioneley's story, even speculations that its sources may be found in the romance genre or in one of the professional companies' repertoires could be excessive. It is, of course, entirely possible that the play was of local or even of Shann origin, inspired by or adapted from something of the immense reading which his commonplace book documents. Whatever its source, whatever its content, its record survives as yet another fascinating variation of the means by which parishes raised community funds and spirits.

Notes

1 Nikolas Pevsner, *Yorkshire: The West Riding*, Harmondsworth, Penguin, 1967², pp. 363-66.

2 All of the remaining information about this play is taken from the commonplace book of Richard Shann of Methley (1561-1627), now British Library Add. MS. 38,599, fols. 71r-v. Shann kept the notebook from about 1585 until his death by 'a consuming consumption', which is noted by his son, Thomas, who continues the family 'Christnings, mariages, and Burialls' section. Richard was a botanist, astrologer, herbalist, surgeon, classicist and musician: the commonplace book includes his observations on these and other subjects, among which are 'Certaine pretie songes hereafter follownge Drawn together, by Richard Shanne 1611'. The book, some 154 folios, merits the complete publication intended by the present author for these songs alone, many of which are local compositions with both lyrics and notation, but the book additionally is remarkable as the intellectual and social record of a sixteenth-century York-

shire gentleman.

3   These observations originally were delivered as a paper in the conference session 'Perspectives on Parish Drama: The North' at the 28th International Congress on Medieval Studies (Kalamazoo, Michigan, May 1993), where they provoked a lively discussion on other potential correspondences between 'romance' and 'drama'. The Methley 'romance drama' ultimately may not prove to be unique, but to date no antecedent has been suggested.

4   Richard Shann married Ann Burton, daughter of Richard Burton alias Carver on 9 June 1588. Their son, Thomas (who finishes the commonplace book genealogy), was born 1 January 1588/9; Ann died 'of dropsie' and was buried on 14 May 1591. Richard subsequently married Marie Chamber, daughter of Richard Chamber of Great Preston, on 30 October 1592; by her he had a daughter, Ann, on 25 June 1595, who is noted in the Methley rushbearing account. Presumably, the 'Burton' family actors were Richard's relatives by his first marriage.

5   The role of women performers continues to undergo reassessment as the Records of Early English Drama project continues. What seems evident at this juncture is that different geographical areas exhibit significant differences: the Devon and Somerset records document female actors and entertainers, as well as female churchwardens; whereas with the exception of a 1469 Wistow Summer Queen the West Riding records document none.

6   This list is not yet completely compiled for the West Riding *Records of Early English Drama* volume, but thus far it includes the following companies with their date of documented performance in parentheses; needless to say, there are lacunae in the records, which thus should be considered as minimal rather than exhaustive: King Henry VI (1450); Duke of York (1450); Lord Plumpton (1456); John Harrington (1480); Lord Eure (1480); Sir E. Hastings (1480); Sir J. Selbayne (1480); King Edward IV (1480); Lord Fitzhugh (1480); Lord Lovell (1480); Earl of Westmorland (1480); Lord Tyrell (1481); Duke of Gloucester (1481); Lord Scroop (1481); Lord Percy (1481); King Henry VII (1496); Bishop of Carlisle (1496); Lord Darcy (1496); Prince Arthur (1500); Earl of Northumberland (1500); Queen Elizabeth of York (1500); Lord Percy (1522); Sir William Ascot (1526); Lord Darby (1526); Sir William Gascoigne (1526); King Henry VIII (1528); Lord Denbroke (1552); Lord Mounteagle (1574); Sir Henry Lee (1574); Earl of Leicester (1574); Queen Elizabeth I (1574); Earl of Worcester (1582); Lord Hunsden (1582); Lord Dudley (1608); Lord Shandoy (1608); Lord Ogle (1609); Queen Anne (1614); Earl of Dorset (1614); Earl of Sussex (1614); Lady Elizabeth (1617); Children of the Revels (1620); King

James (1620); Bradshaw (1627); Kempton (1627); Mr. Swinerton (1627); King Charles I (1629); Earl of Derby (1629); Revels (1631); Mr. Parie (1632); Queen Henrietta Maria (1632).

7   British Library Add. MS. 38,599, fol. 88.

8. Sir Philip Sidney, in his digression on the state of contemporary English poetry in *The Defence of Poesy*. See, e.g.: Hyder Rollins and Herschel Baker, *The Renaissance in England*, Boston, D. C. Heath, 1954, p. 621.

J.R. SIMPSON:

Animal Body, Literary Corpus
The Old French *Roman de Renart*

Amsterdam/Atlanta, GA 1996. 242 pp.
(Faux Titre 110)
ISBN: 90-5183-976-6   Hfl. 75,-/US-$ 50.-

Contents: Acknowledgments. Guide to references. Introduction. Chapter One: Sin, History and Monkeys. Chapter Two: Sexuality and Its Consequences: The Rape of Hersent and its Renarrations. Chapter Three: Liminality. Chapter Four: Law and Government. Chapter Five: Recapitulation. Conclusions. Appendix One: Note on Editions and Branch Titles. Bibliography. Index.

USA/Canada: Editions Rodopi B.V., 2015 South Park Place, Atlanta, GA 30339, Tel. (770) 933-0027, *Call toll-free* (U.S. only) 1-800-225- 3998, Fax (770) 933-9644, *E-mail:* F.van.der.Zee@rodopi.nl
All Other Countries: Editions Rodopi B.V., Keizersgracht 302-304, 1016 EX Amsterdam, The Netherlands. Tel. + + 31 (0)20-622-75-07, Fax + + 31 (0)20-638-09-48, *E-mail:* F.van.der.Zee@rodopi.nl

JEERING DREAMERS
Villiers de l'Isle-Adam's
L'Eve Future at our Fin de Siècle

A Collection of Essays edited by John Anzalone
Preface by Alain Raitt

Amsterdam/Atlanta, GA 1996. 210 pp.
(Faux Titre 111)
ISBN: 90-5183-939-1   Hfl. 60,-/US-$ 40.-

USA/Canada: Editions Rodopi B.V., 2015 South Park Place, Atlanta, GA 30339, Tel. (770) 933-0027, *Call toll-free* (U.S. only) 1-800-225- 3998, Fax (770) 933-9644, *E-mail:* F.van.der.Zee@rodopi.nl
All Other Countries: Editions Rodopi B.V., Keizersgracht 302-304, 1016 EX Amsterdam, The Netherlands. Tel. + + 31 (0)20-622-75-07, Fax + + 31 (0)20-638-09-48, *E-mail:* F.van.der.Zee@rodopi.nl